THE **NEW FOREST** COMPANION
A Walker's Guide

THE NEW FOREST COMPANION

A Walker's Guide

ANNE-MARIE EDWARDS

ARCADY BOOKS

Ashurst, Southampton

First edition 1987

ARCADY BOOKS LTD
2 Woodlands Road
Ashurst
Southampton
Hampshire SO4 2AD

All rights reserved. No part of this publication may be reproduced, stored in a retrieval system or transmitted, in any form, or by any means, electronic, mechanical, photocopying, recording or otherwise, without the prior permission of the publishers.

© Anne-Marie Edwards 1987

ISBN 0 907753 11 6

Maps drawn by Julie Edwards, based on Ordnance Survey Maps with the permission of the Controller of Her Majesy's Stationery Office. Crown Copyright reserved.

Design and line drawings by Louise Burston

Phototypeset by Pauline Newton

Printed by Villiers Publications Ltd, 26a Shepherds Hill, London N6 5AH

· ACKNOWLEDGEMENTS ·

It is a pleasure to thank all the people I have met on my travels who talked to me about the Forest. My thanks also to Mr and Mrs Hugh Pasmore who lent me books, Mr John Chapman of the Forestry Commission and the Reverend Ben Eliot and Mr and Mrs Michael Stokes who gave me valuable information about the north of the Forest. I would like to thank the ever-helpful staffs of Southampton, Totton, Hythe and Bournemouth Public Libraries.

Quotations from *Hampshire Days*, *Remarks on Forest Scenery*, *Rural Rides* and *It Happened in Hampshire* are by kind permission of the publishers.

I would like to thank Pauline Newton for her patient typesetting and Louise Burston who designed the book and helped in every stage of its production. I shall always be grateful to my friend and neighbour, Margaret, who was the first to suggest I should record my walks, and Mary, the best of companions, for her constant support. Finally I thank my daughter Julie who drew the maps with so much care, and my husband Mike who makes everything possible.

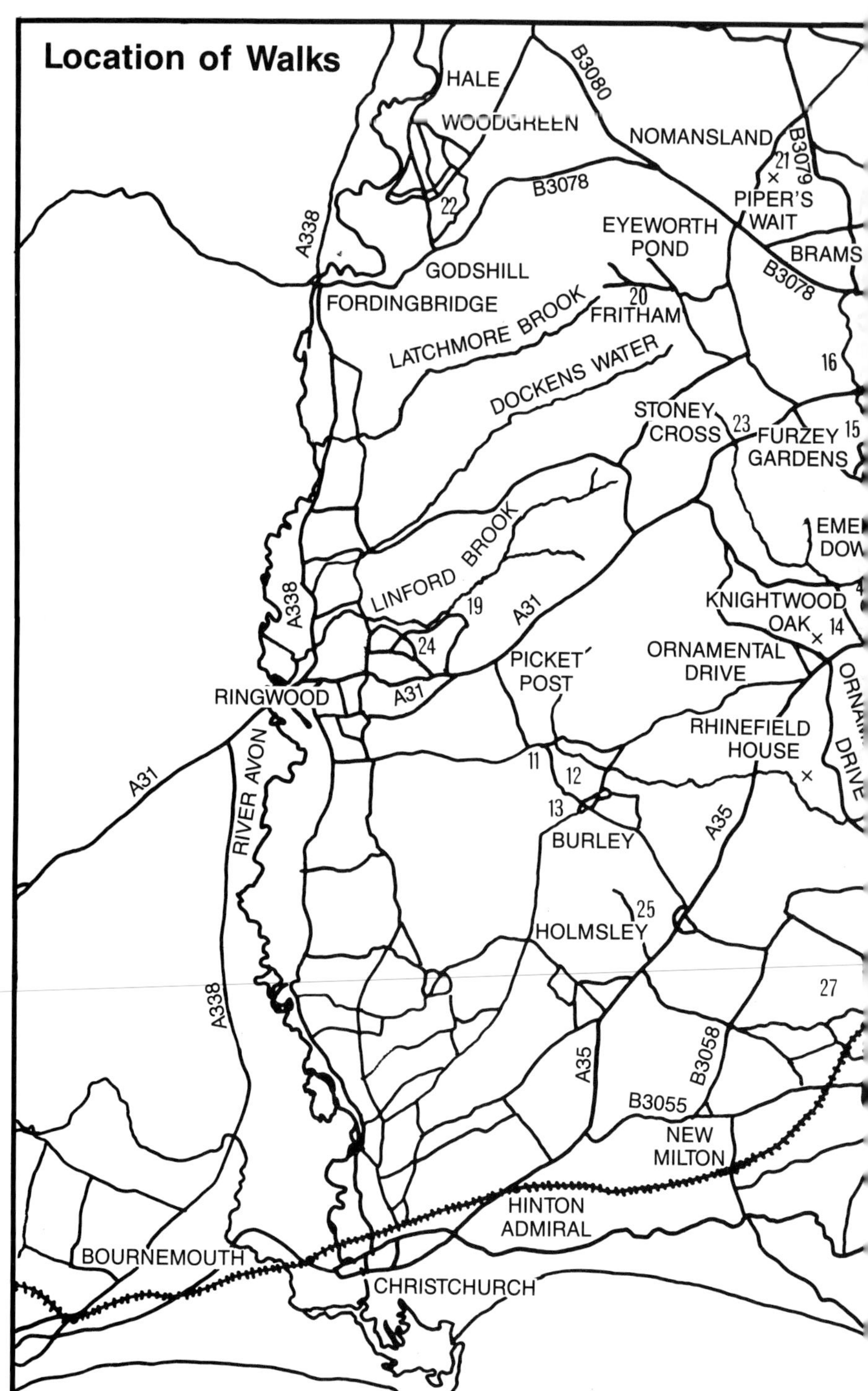

Location of Walks
HALE
WOODGREEN
B3080
NOMANSLAND
B3079
21
PIPER'S WAIT
B3078
22
EYEWORTH POND
BRAMS
B3078
A338
GODSHILL
20
FRITHAM
16
FORDINGBRIDGE
LATCHMORE BROOK
DOCKENS WATER
STONEY CROSS
23
FURZEY GARDENS
15
EME DOW
LINFORD BROOK
19
A31
KNIGHTWOOD OAK
14
A338
24
PICKET POST
ORNAMENTAL DRIVE
ORNA DRIVE
RINGWOOD
A31
A31
RHINEFIELD HOUSE
A31
11
12
13
A35
RIVER AVON
BURLEY
25
A35
HOLMSLEY
27
A338
B3058
B3055
NEW MILTON
HINTON ADMIRAL
BOURNEMOUTH
CHRISTCHURCH

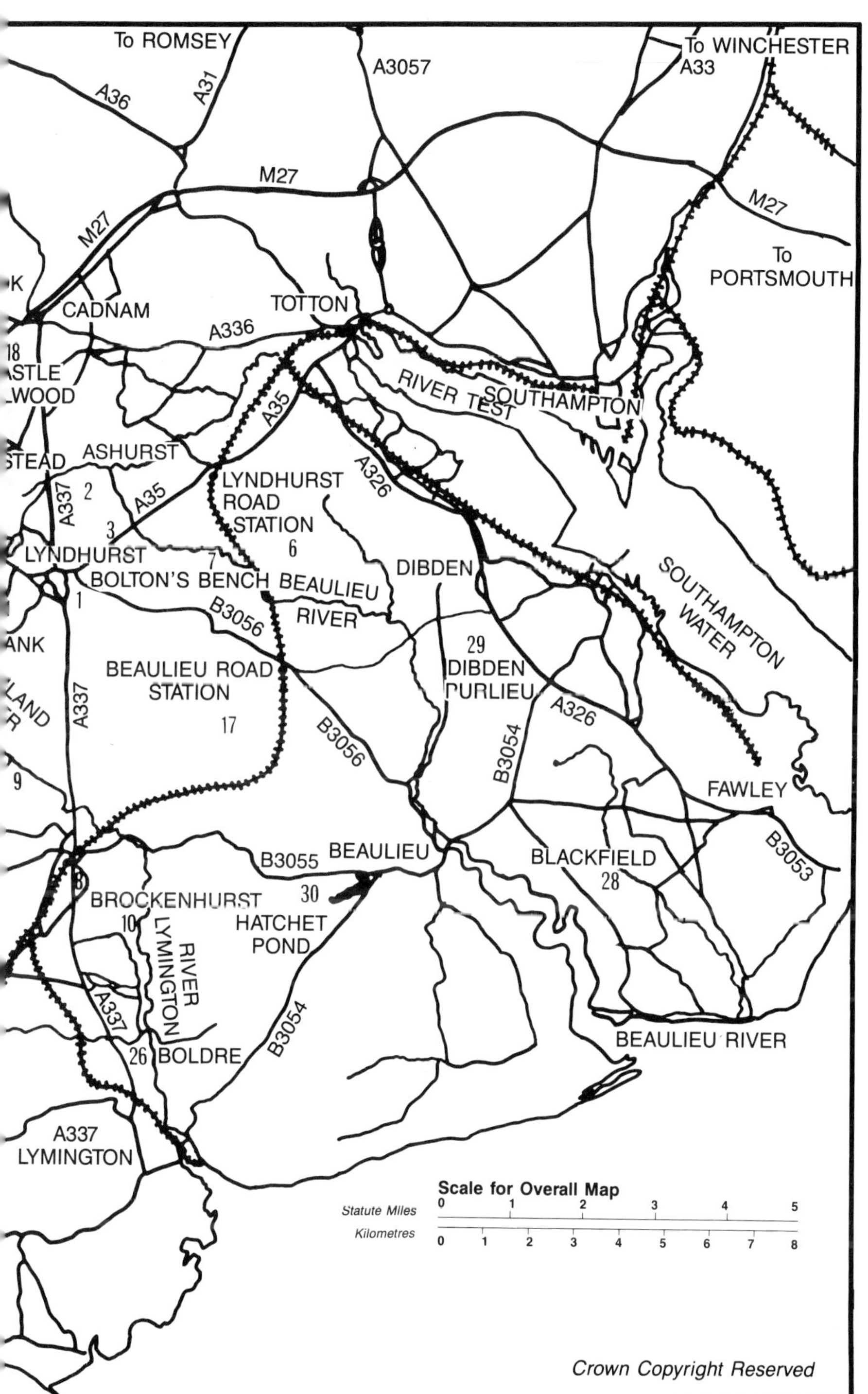

To ROMSEY
To WINCHESTER
A33
A3057
A36
A31
M27
M27
To PORTSMOUTH
M27
CADNAM
TOTTON
A336
RIVER TEST
SOUTHAMPTON
18
ASTLE
WOOD
A35
STEAD
ASHURST
A326
2
A35
LYNDHURST
ROAD
STATION
6
A337
3
DIBDEN
SOUTHAMPTON
WATER
LYNDHURST
7
BOLTON'S BENCH
BEAULIEU
RIVER
B3056
ANK
1
29
DIBDEN
PURLIEU
BEAULIEU ROAD
STATION
LAND
R
A337
17
B3056
A326
B3054
9
FAWLEY
B3056
BEAULIEU
BLACKFIELD
B3053
B3055
28
BROCKENHURST
30
10
HATCHET
POND
RIVER LYMINGTON
A337
B3054
BEAULIEU RIVER
26
BOLDRE
A337
LYMINGTON
Scale for Overall Map
Statute Miles
0   1   2   3   4   5
Kilometres
0 1 2 3 4 5 6 7 8
Crown Copyright Reserved

• GENERAL MAP KEY •

—— *Road*
++++ *Railway*
------- *Footpath*
+ *Church*
BS *Bus Stop*
P *Parking*
CS *Campsite*
→ *Route of Walk*
⇉ *Alternative route*
⇥ *Route from Bus Stop*
⊓⊓⊓⊓ *New Forest Boundary*
++++ *Inclosure Boundary*
░░ *Woodland Area*

• CONTENTS •

• ABOUT THE FOREST •

The New Forest in Hampshire is one of the most beautiful areas of countryside in Britain. It is also a unique example of a medieval hunting forest which has survived into our own times and is still the property of the Crown. For, from 1079, when William the Conqueror declared the wild country stretching from Southampton Water to the Avon valley and from the Wiltshire Downs to the Solent his own special hunting ground, no one has been able to farm the Forest without the monarch's permission. Of course, encroachments have been made over the centuries, but today over a hundred square miles of often still-medieval forest remain, criss-crossed by a multitude of tracks that lead through oak and beech woods whose trees have provided the timber for Britain's 'wooden walls', as well as through the newer pine woods planted to help the Forest pay its way in the twentieth century. It is a forest in the true medieval sense, only partly covered by trees. Lovely paths dip across the river valleys and over wide heaths, fragrant with the scent of gorse and heather.

Follow these ways deep into the Forest and you will discover much to reward you. But I think the Forest's greatest glory is what the Forestry Commission term the 'ancient and ornamental' woodlands. These are the oldest woods of oak and beech trees, many of them cut short, or pollarded at an early period of growth. As this custom was declared illegal in 1698, many of these great trees must be up to four hundred years old. Without their heads, their main trunks have sprouted several stems which now, wreathed with ivy and often set with little gardens of ferns, spread massive arms far over the Forest floor. One of the rambles in this book takes you to the oldest oak tree of all, the Knightwood oak, through glades of mighty trees which are the home of the purple emperor butterfly and in whose shadow blooms the wild gladiolus.

These woods, particularly where oaks predominate, are loved by all wild creatures. You will see fallow deer with their spreading antlers, the smaller reddish-brown roe, the little spotted sika and if you are lucky, a red deer stag guarding his harem of hinds with their floppy ears and large eloquent eyes. Badgers and foxes follow their own tracks through the undergrowth. The return of the rabbit in large numbers has brought the buzzard back to hover over the tree tops on his great oblong wings. Along the banks of the Beaulieu river you will still hear the song of nightingales and brilliant flashes of blue and green betray the presence of kingfishers over the Forest streams.

Out on the heath too, there are sounds and scents to haunt your memory: larks soaring and singing even on grey days, heather and gorse smelling as rich as honey, the sharp tang of the gold-withey (or bog myrtle) as you brush past it by the streams. You will be rewarded by spreading views, west over the Avon valley to the Wiltshire Downs, south to the curving line of the Isle of Wight hills. And here you will feel close to the Forest's history as you pass tumuli or burial mounds raised by Britons a thousand years before the birth of Christ, and climb the embankments of Iron Age forts which dominated the hill tops when the Romans landed.

And you will discover the meaning of the law of the Forest. In order to survive, the people who lived close to the Forest had to be granted certain rights. They were allowed to pasture their ponies, cattle, donkeys and geese in the Forest, and, during the pannage season in Autumn when the acorns and beech seeds (mast) had fallen, they could turn out their pigs. Other rights included permission to gather firewood, cut peat, and spread marl dug from pits in the Forest to improve the quality of their land. These rights were attached to certain houses. Today, the people who live in those houses, the Commoners, exercise their rights as vigorously as ever. They own the famous ponies, rounding them up at various times of the year for marking and sale with scenes reminiscent of the Wild West. For these tough, shaggy ponies, only found in the New Forest, have not forgotten their wild ancestry. They look docile but, like any wild creature, head for cover the moment they suspect their freedom is threatened. Their tempers too are uncertain and it is dangerous, however appealing they look, to feed them.

If you buy or rent a house in the Forest, you can check whether you have 'rights of common' in an atlas kept in the office of the Clerk to the verderers in Lymington. The verderers are officials of the ancient Forest court, still meeting regularly to settle local differences in the original courthouse in Lyndhurst, the Forest capital. The court is open to all and well worth a visit.

The Forest is quiet now, possibly quieter than at any other time in its long history. In the past we would meet the people who lived and worked here, all dependent to some extent, on the Forest. We would meet gypsies, charcoal-burners, wood-cutters, snake-catchers, swineherds, perhaps even smugglers! They have all gone yet the Forest holds their story still. As we walk, we hear some of that story, and other more strange tales from the Forest's wealth of folklore.

We follow a ridgeway deep into the great woods around Lyndhurst, take a smuggler's track to an ancient hill fort at Burley, come across Gritnam, a tiny hamlet in a Forest clearing that could have arrived straight out of the *Domesday Book*, visit Castle Malwood where William the Conqueror's favourite son, William Rufus, feasted the night before his fatal hunting expedition, and walk round Canterton close to the stone that marks the spot where, according to tradition, he fell from his horse with an arrow through his heart. We explore 'Churchplace' — one of several in the Forest — possibly the site of a Saxon village destroyed by William, and look at the origin of Woodgreen's 'Merry Sundays'. We climb Bishop's Dyke and wonder why a medieval Bishop should wish to own a patch of the Forest's marshland.

I hope you will feel tempted to try these walks and rediscover this wonderful part of our heritage. Of one thing you can be sure. However often you may walk even a familiar way, you will never tire of the New Forest. With its changing colours, its hazy, shimmering distances, its dappled effects of light and shade, it is never the same from one day to the next. The Forest remains a continually unfolding source of delight.

• ON FOOT IN THE FOREST •

At all seasons of the year the Forest will delight you. It has a subtle charm all its own. There are no awe-inspiring cliffs, waterfalls or mountains, just an overall gentle loveliness that will captivate you the more you walk its quiet ways. You will gather a host of unforgettable impressions — beech buds unfolding their first silky leaves, huge oaks spreading the full weight of their summer foliage over sunlit glades, the velvet softness of a Forest lawn, the scent of gorse on the heath, the grace of a roe deer surprised down a ride, a leggy foal nuzzling his mother for comfort in a world too new for him — to name only a few of them.

All this beauty is waiting for us but sometimes it can be surprisingly difficult to get away from the bustle of the crowded centres and discover it! The Forest is so old; so many people have lived and worked here that the whole area is a labyrinth of paths. A wide, embanked way made to support woodcutters' carts can, today, literally vanish at your feet. There are no signposts and one wood can look very much like another. If you have left a car, you must get back to it! So I have devised this book as a series of safe family walks, all roughly circular, with starting points accessible by car and public transport. They are not the frequented ways, but my own favourite walks; each of them showing a different aspect of the Forest's beauty or its history. An exception is the Forestry Commission's Ober Water Trail which I have included as a lovely example of these pleasant walks.

When you are out in the Forest it is always wise to walk with a map that shows the whole area. I recommend the Ordnance Survey Outdoor Leisure Map. The scale is ideal, 1:25000 (4 cm to 1 km or about 2½ inches to 1 mile). If you buy a plastic case to put it in it won't flap about irritatingly in windy weather.

But Forest paths occasionally defeat even the map-makers and if you are walking without directions and want to be really safe, certain of your path and sure it is continuing to take you in the right direction, then you must carry a compass. I prefer the SILVA compass recommended by rambling associations which is small, light and easy to use. The leaflet that comes with it explains how to use it in detail.

The problem of what to wear on your feet is easily solved. However dry the Forest may appear there is sure to be a boggy patch lurking somewhere. You need strong, waterproof shoes or boots. Unless I am following known gravel tracks or the Forestry Commission's Trails, I wear a pair of ordinary wellingtons — they keep my feet and ankles dry and fend off mud splashes. But for a really long walk or when the Forest is very wet I wear light boots with Vibram soles which give a better grip. I usually try to remember to carry some sticking plasters to use at the first hint of a blister.

Sometimes you can start your walk in the shelter of woodland to emerge onto the heath to find a surprisingly cold wind blowing. Take a windproof anorak with a hood and an extra woolly if you think you might need it, and a pair of warm gloves. I find a light mackintosh that folds and stows easily quite sufficient.

Even if you do not plan a full-scale picnic, it is wise to take a supply of sustaining food on all Forest expeditions. My family's usual lifesavers include fruit and nut bars, chocolate, fruit cake — the richer the better, extra calories are good for walkers! — and apples. A drink is useful too. You can buy small plastic flasks with flattened sides which will fit comfortably into a haversack. They are cheap and light and the tops double as cups.

Two more hints on Forest walking. I have found from experience that Forest bogs, identifiable by waving tufts of cotton grass, are best avoided even if it means a detour. If you are in doubt, keep to the heather, or ground under trees, and look for animal tracks round them; deer don't like getting their feet wet. There is no need to worry about snakes. There are adders (V-markings down their backs) but they are much more terrified of you than you are of them and will quickly get out of your way. However, if you are unfortunate enough to be bitten go as quickly as possible to the nearest hospital. Anti-snake serum is kept at Lyndhurst, Southampton, Hythe, Lymington and the Royal Victoria at Boscombe.

Note: *Although we can wander freely in the Forest, the Forestry Commission has a duty to make it pay its way. So protect our good name and the national interest by shutting all gates and avoiding any risk of fire. Outside the Forest boundaries, every care has been taken to follow rights of way or paths to which the public has been granted access. However, these are liable to change for which the author cannot be held responsible.*

· LYNDHURST ·

There is no better way to introduce yourself to the New Forest than to spend some time exploring the Forest's ancient administrative 'capital', Lyndhurst. In spite of the crowds and the traffic that often jams its narrow High Street it is a true Forest village still, worthy of its position and rich in tradition. To appreciate Lyndhurst you must approach the village on foot through the Forest. Come from the west through Bank, or from the east over Bolton's Bench and your first impression will be the right one — a lonely church spire encircled by trees. As you come closer, using the spire as your guide, even today it is easy to imagine the village as it must have always looked to the traveller: a cluster of friendly lights in the centre of a beautiful but inhospitable wilderness.

New Forest churches are built on hills if possible to serve as landmarks and Lyndhurst's parish church of St Michael and All Angels stands at a high point in the village, overlooking the main street. It has a lovely east window designed by Burne Jones and in the churchyard you will find the grave of Mrs Hargreaves, the 'Alice' of Lewis Carroll's *Alice in Wonderland*. Next to the church is the Queen's House. There has been a royal manor here since the tenth century and the present elegant house was largely rebuilt by Charles II. It is now the home of the Forestry Commission. Under the same roof is the Verderer's Court dating back to the fourteenth century. In Norman times the Verderers had to administer the terribly harsh Forest laws and the court still meets today to settle the claims and disputes of the Commoners. Facing the courtroom is one of Lyndhurst's old seventeenth century coaching inns, The Crown.

Lyndhurst combines historic charm with care for its visitors. There are plenty of good restaurants and cafés and a wide choice of accommodation. Close to the High Street, in the centre of the village, is a large free car park. Here you will find an excellent Information Centre where you can obtain help and advice on all aspects of the Forest.

Leave the busy High Street and follow some of the little lanes and you will find, as with all Forest villages, the houses seem to merge into the woodlands and heaths. There are no strict boundaries. Lyndhurst is both in the Forest and of it: medieval still in that it is so much a part of its surroundings.

Walk 1

PONDHEAD INCLOSURE AND BOLTON'S BENCH

Starting point: Lyndhurst central car park.

Distance: 2 miles.

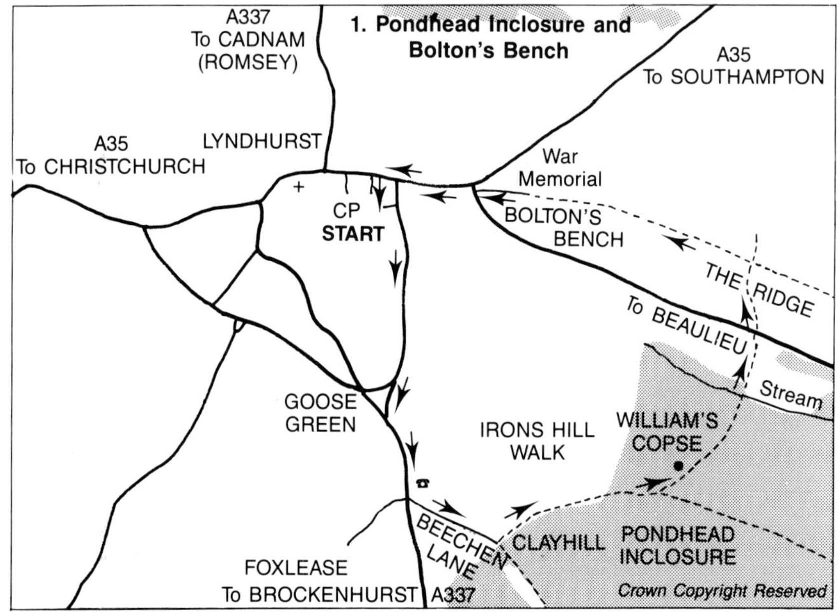

Additions to Key:
CP Lyndhurst central car park
☎ *Telephone box*

For general Key see p. viii

This is an easy, leisurely stroll suitable for everyone. There is a good, well-drained path all the way round — level enough for pushchairs — so it is ideal if you have small children or older people in your group. And it is really surprising how much of the Forest's varied scenery of oak and beech woods and open heathland you can enjoy with very little effort!

There are three possible exits for walkers from Lyndhurst's central car park. Do not take either of the routes leading to the High Street but walk past the 'No Entry' signs along the lane that leads you to the A337, the Lyndhurst–Lymington road. (It is directly ahead of you if you stand with your back to the Community Centre.) Turn right and follow the road in the direction of Lymington. You come to a grassy area, Goose Green. Keep straight on here still in the direction of Lymington. You pass a 'phone box on your left then come to a minor road, Beechen Lane, on your left. It is opposite the drive leading to Foxlease House, the Girl Guides' Association Training Centre. Turn left down Beechen Lane and ahead you will see the tall oaks and beeches of Pondhead Inclosure. As you approach the Inclosure you will see a cattle grid. Turn left before the grid to cross another cattle grid and continue along a delightful woodland path.

Now you are really in the Forest. The path is shaded by oaks and beeches, their ivy-darkened trunks rising from dense thickets of holly. Through the trees on your left you will see Lyndhurst church spire. Follow this lovely path as it leads you between Irons Hill Walk and Clayhill. The path bears right to take you into Pondhead Inclosure and then divides. Take the left-hand path and after about a hundred yards look to the left of the path for an interesting memorial. In 1979 the New Forest celebrated nine hundred years as a Royal Forest. You will see a plaque on a hollowed wooden support in front of a special area designated 'William's Copse'. The plaque reads: 'Nine hundred Sessile Oaks were planted here in 1979 to commemorate the creation of the New Forest by William I in 1079. May it contribute to the sylvan pleasures of our successors.'

Our path leads over a wooden bridge across a stream to a gate and stile. Cross over and keep straight ahead to the minor road running from Lyndhurst to Beaulieu. Go over the road to the path you will see ahead running past a Forestry Commission barrier. The path rises to bring you high on the heath to the east of Lyndhurst. Here you have wide views over the Forest heathlands, especially eastwards to the great woods of Matley and Denny. Follow the path for a few yards to a crossing path and turn left in the direction of Lyndhurst church spire.

Continue along the ridge and soon you will see the mound topped with a clump of trees known as Bolton's Bench a little to your left. This earthwork possibly dates back to the Iron Age and is named after Lord Bolton who was Lord Warden of the Forest in 1688. Pass Bolton's Bench on your left and the War Memorial on your right. The path becomes a metalled road which brings you down to the foot of Lyndhurst High Street. Walk up the High Street and turn left down the A337 Lyndhurst–Lymington road. The entry to the car park is the first lane on your right.

Walk 2

FOLDSGATE INCLOSURE AND FAIR CROSS VALLEY

Starting point: Lyndhurst central car park.

Distance: 2½ miles.

This walk takes you north of Lyndhurst to enjoy some of the Forest woods and heaths crossed by the Romsey Road. Although it is only two and a half miles round there is a surprising variety of scenery.

From the car park take one of the exits that lead you to the High Street. Turn left and walk up to the junction with the Romsey road where there is a set of traffic lights. Cross the High Street and follow the Romsey Road. Just past a road on the left called 'Forest Gardens' you will see a footpath on the left running uphill almost parallel with the main road at first. Follow the path as it runs to the right of a green. When the path bends right keep straight on along a narrow path that brings you down to a lane with the main road quite close on the right. Walk on along the lane past 'The Waterloo Arms' and over the junction of Pikes Hill Avenue

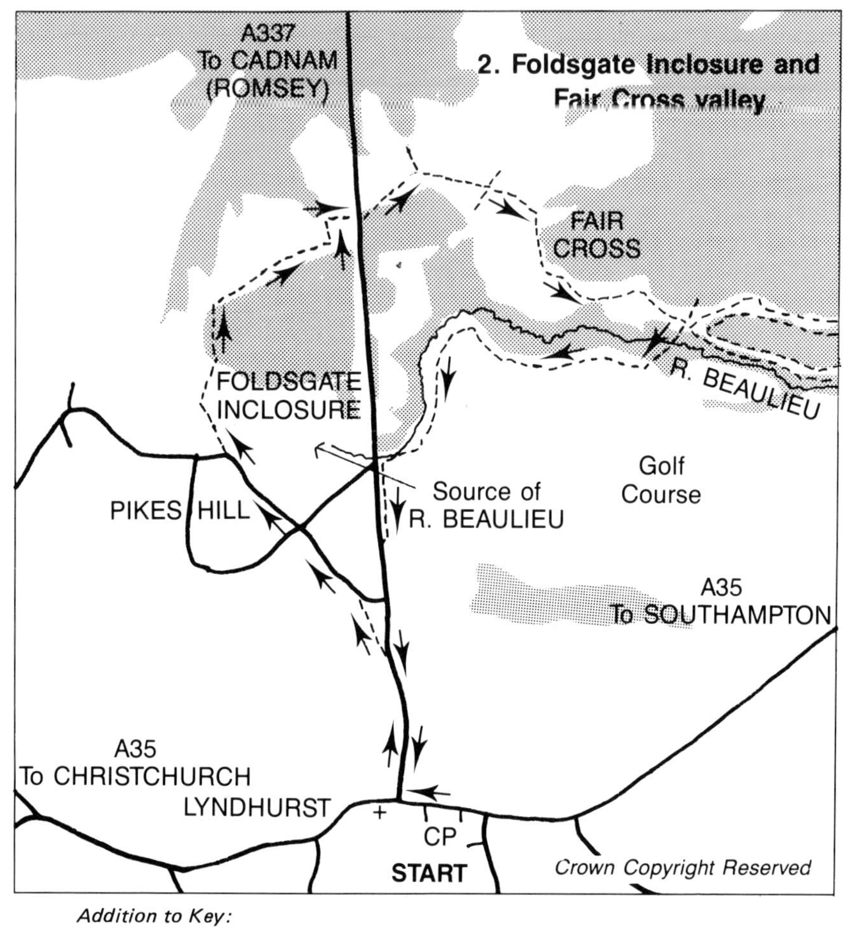

Addition to Key:
CP Lyndhurst central car park

For general Key see p. viii

and Broughton Road. The road brings you to a cattle grid and turns left. Keep straight on here across the cattle grid and follow the path over the green. Now you leave the village behind and you are really in the Forest among tall oak and beech trees. Go past a Forestry Commission barrier and bear right, following the path over a grassy heath towards Foldsgate Inclosure: a tempting little wood of oaks, beeches and chestnuts. As you enter the wood and cross the embankment that marks the Inclosure boundary our path bears left towards the northern edge of Foldsgate. Keep to the woodland path as it follows the curve of the Inclosure close to the boundary embankment with the tree-covered hill on your right. The path leads you out of the wood onto a heath. Do not follow the path as it leads straight ahead over the heath but turn right and walk towards the Romsey road with the Inclosure close on your right. There is a very narrow path to follow. When you are about fifty yards from the road you come to a crosstrack. Turn left along this for just a few yards and you will see a gate on your right leading to the road.

Go through the gate, across the main road and through the gate which is a little to your left on the other side.

Follow the path from the gate slightly uphill over a lovely heath dotted with silver birches. A path joins our way from the left and continues right. Bear right along this over a wide heath ringed with the dark outlines of woods. Go straight over a cross track towards a wood. Just before you reach the trees you meet a crossing path. Bear right and follow the white path as it dips and curves south-east along the hillside at Fair Cross. This is a beautiful place. As you follow the little path along the hillside above a shallow valley full of the Forest's subtle contrasts of light and shade it is hard to believe that the busy Romsey Road is only five minutes away!

The path falls a little and ahead you will see the curve of a wide greenway. Before the greenway you come to a crosstrack. Turn right, a little downhill, and walk down to a belt of trees. These fringe a stream — an infant Beaulieu river. Cross the bridge and you leave the trees to emerge on the northern edge of Lyndhurst golf course. Straight ahead, over the green you will see the spire of Lyndhurst church. Turn right and walk round the edge of the golf course, keeping the trees close on your right and bearing left as you approach the Romsey Road. Do not go through the first gate to the road. It is more pleasant to continue with the fence on your right a little further to a stile before joining the road. Or you may prefer to walk on to a gate at the other end of the golf course which you will see a little to your left. Walk back up the road into the village and turn left for the car park.

Walk 3

LYNDHURST TO ASHURST: A WALKER'S WAY

Starting point: Lyndhurst central car park.

Distance: Seven miles all the way round. This walk can easily be divided into two by making use of the bus service between Lyndhurst and Ashurst.

Campsite: Ashurst. This village is the half-way point so the circular walk can be started here.

The great historian of the Forest, John Wise, said in his book *The New Forest*, first published in 1883, that the people of Lyndhurst 'ought to be the happiest and most contented in England, for they possess a wider park and nobler trees than even Royalty'. He could say the same today. If you arrive in the bustling little Forest capital during a busy summer weekend you might find this difficult to believe! However, a few minutes walk away the quiet glades and soft green lawns of the Forest are waiting for you to discover. This circular walk to Ashurst and back will take you through some of the most lovely parts of the Forest showing all its contrasts of woods and heathlands.

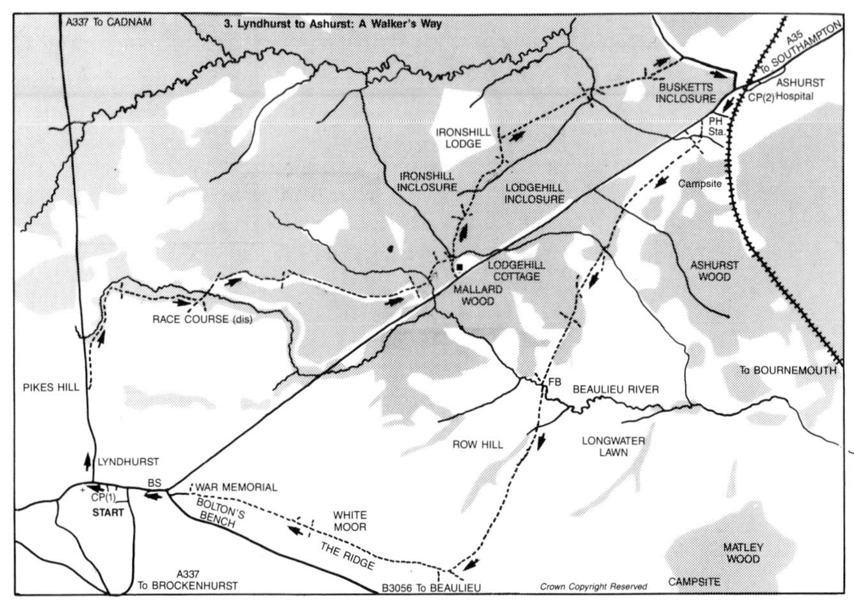

Additions to Key:

CP(1)	*Lyndhurst central car park*	Sta	*Lyndhurst Road Station (Ashurst)*
CP (2)	*Ashurst car park*	Hosp	*Ashurst Hospital*
FB	*Footbridge*		
PH	*New Forest Inn*		*For general Key see p. viii*

The walk is about seven miles round but if you wish you can divide the walk into two and catch the bus back to Lyndhurst from Ashurst, the half-way point. Like Lyndhurst, Ashurst has excellent restaurants and cafés.

From the car park in Lyndhurst walk the few yards past the Information Centre to the High Street. Turn left up the hill towards the church but before you get there, at the traffic lights, turn right down the Romsey Road. Walk on down the hill across the top of the road 'Racecourse View'. (We shall be following part of the former racecourse.) When you see 'Pikes Hill' sign on your left, look for a small wooden stile (the step-over variety) leading onto the green on your right. Cross the stile and turn immediately left with the railings on your left along a narrow path. Our way is along the edge of the golf course keeping close to the fringe of woodland. You pass a gate leading into the woods on your left then bear right, keeping the fringe of trees close on your left so skirting the golf course. Our path now bears right over a track. Keep on along the edge of the woods until you come to a good path leading left into the trees. If you look right, over the golf course, you will see the spire of Lyndhurst Church in line with our path.

Turn left and follow the path across a small footbridge over an infant Beaulieu river. The river rises at Pikes Hill in Lyndhurst. The path quickly brings you out of the trees bordering the stream. On your right you will see a curve in a wide green way. Turn right towards a wooden post supporting the wire rails marking the boundary of this green way. Enter the green way by the post and bear left along this beautiful woodland path.

Your way becomes even more lovely as it goes deeper into ancient woods, its soft green turf supporting groups of silver birches and an occasional solitary picturesque pine. I walked here in late July which is a special time in the Forest for orchids. I found several of these exotic-looking flowers beside the path including the delicate white lesser butterfly orchid. The flowers really do resemble butterflies. It was a little early to see many butterflies themselves though some did flutter around my feet. Two of the many species you will find in the Forest are the white admiral and the silver-washed fritillary. Among the old oaks bordering your way are some pollarded trees spreading their several trunks almost horizontally above the Forest floor.

When you come to a wide crosstrack — look right and you will see a gate leading to the main road, the A35 — go straight over, cross the poles and follow the green path ahead. Leave some wooden buildings near Lodgehill Cottage on your right. Ignore the first main track on your left which leads to a Forestry Commission barrier and continue for a few more yards to a wide gravel crosstrack. (If you look right you will see that it leads to Lodgehill Cottage and the main road.) Turn left and follow the gravel track as it climbs slightly uphill. At the top, by a ramp, keep straight on over a crossing track, slightly downhill along the gravel. Until recent times all the Forest roads were gravel, changing their colour with the light; golden in the sun and silver under the moon.

Go straight over the next crosstrack. Keep straight on for just a few yards, then turn right down a wide gravel track opposite a small wooden gate leading to Iron-shill Lodge. Walk down the ride until you come to a crosstrack. The gravel path curves left. Cross over and follow the path almost opposite for a few yards. Now the path divides. Keep on down the left hand of the two paths. This path is roughly parallel with the A35 which is on your right though not visible.

You pass a boggy area rimmed with an embankment planted with pines. This was once a pond and I was told by Mr Green, a local keeper, that he remembered skating parties coming through the Forest from nearby Ashurst Lodge when the pond was frozen over. They would arrive with torches and hampers to skate by moonlight. It must have been a noisy, lively scene but now the former pond is a rather strange marsh, full of twisted trees struggling to survive.

Ignore the first green ride you pass on your left but turn left down the second which leads you to a gate opening into Woodlands Road. Turn right and follow the path over the grassy lawn beside the road. Follow the road as it turns right to meet the A35. Just over the bridge on your left you will find shops and cafés and an excellent pub, the Happy Cheese. Over the road and a little to your right you will find another place for a good meal and a pint — with a playground for the children — the New Forest Inn. This old inn was originally built as a hunting lodge and was visited by Queen Victoria. From Ashurst you can catch a Lymington or Bournemouth bus back to Lyndhurst if you wish.

To continue our walk cross the A35 at the top of Woodlands Road and turn right past the New Forest Inn towards the gate leading to Ashurst campsite. Go through the gate but do not follow the road to the site. Instead, turn right and make your way over the grass and heath with the campsite on your left and the main road about three hundred yards away on your right. There is no clear track at this point but just walk straight ahead roughly parallel with the main road. Soon you will see a small wood on your right between you and the road. Walk along the fringe of the wood with the wood on your right. This is a relic of an ancient wood and some magnificent pollarded trees survive, all with their anklets of holly and trunks and branches heavily draped with ivy and honeysuckle. Cross straight over the lane to Ashurst Lodge and keep walking straight ahead past a Forestry Commission barrier. Now you will be able to follow a path which winds through woods and over small heaths looking as remote today as in the time of William the Conqueror. Just after you cross a footbridge over a ditch our path divides. Ignore the path bearing slightly left and keep straight on over a more open area towards the outlying fringes of Mallard Wood. As you enter the wood, the way becomes a wide, green path. This is one of the Forest's loveliest oak and beech woods, classified by the Forestry Commission as 'ancient and ornamental'. It is the home of many wild creatures including badgers and deer. You come out onto the heath again and now a wide view stretches ahead of you. Across Longwater Lawn you will see our destination: the ridge which is a little to the east of Lyndhurst. Our path leads to a bridge over the Beaulieu river, still only a stream bordered with bog asphodel and starred in June with the white flowers of water crowfoot. Just over the bridge a small stone marks the parish boundary of Colbury. Recently residents of Colbury have walked the boundaries of their parish and published a booklet obtainable in the local shops. Keep straight on along the path which becomes raised and embanked to cross some boggy areas. Here the air is heavy with the pungent scent of the bog myrtle or gold withey. Between the bushes dart turquoise and emerald dragonflies.

The path climbs a little to run to the left of a small hill crowned with pines. Beneath the pines the ground is dry and firm and the air scented. This is a perfect place to pause and enjoy the peace and timeless quality of the Forest. Follow the path as it rises gently towards the ridge. You will see Lyndhurst church spire on your right and a conspicuous white house directly ahead. When you gain the crest of the ridge you will see the Lyndhurst–Beaulieu road, B3056, ahead. Walk towards it but before you reach the road you will meet a wide white track. Turn right and follow this well-marked way in the direction of Lyndhurst church spire. You are now walking along 'The Ridge', part of the boundary of Park Pale which was an area defined as a deer park in 1291. Soon you will see the dome-shaped hill crowned with trees just east of Lyndhurst that features on the village sign. The mound possibly dates back to the Iron Age and is called Bolton's Bench after Lord Bolton who was Lord Warden of the Forest in 1688. You pass a small chapel on your right and the cricket pitch on your left. Our way now becomes a metalled road to lead you past the Bench, to the left of the War Memorial. When you meet the main road turn left to walk up Lyndhurst High Street and so back to the car park.

If you intend doing the whole walk, allow yourself plenty of time and pack some supplies. This is too good to rush!

Walk 4

ACRES DOWN: A RIDGE WALK

Starting point: Swan Green car park, near Lyndhurst. Bus: Swan Green, near Lyndhurst.

Distance: About seven and a half miles all the way round or a shorter circuit of 4 miles.

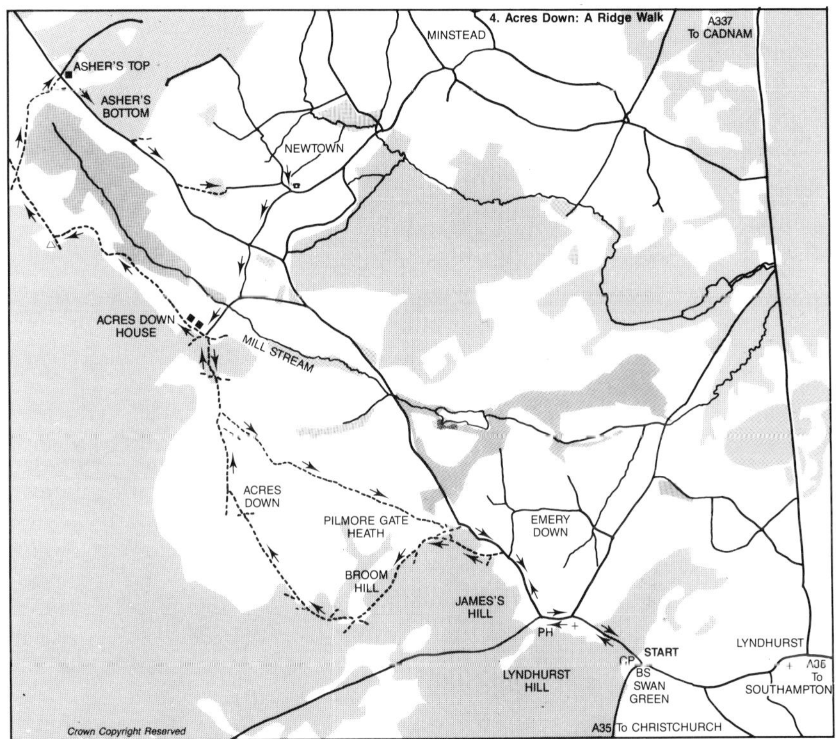

Additions to Key:

CP *Swan Green car park*   △ *Triangulation point*

☎ *Telephone box*   *For general key see p. viii*

PH *New Forest Inn*

Ridge walks are rare in the Forest as it is generally low-lying, but when they do occur they give us rare insights into the Forest's beauty; its contrasting shades of woodlands and wide expanses of quiet heaths. This ridge walk, only two miles from the Forest capital, Lyndhurst, is my favourite. There is no difficult in finding it — no trackless wastes to cross — but it will lead you to the real heart of this wonderful Forest. The distance round is about seven and a half miles but I will suggest also a shorter return route which reduces the distance to about four miles. Allow a full day for the longer walk.

We start from the glorious woods north-west of Lyndhurst, from Swan Green, the hamlet on the A35 Bournemouth road, just west of the Forest capital. It's so close you can walk from Lyndhurst or catch the bus from Southampton. Walk up the road towards Bournemouth for a few yards then turn right at Swan Green along the road to Emery Down. If you arrive by car, park in the Swan Green car park which is on the left of the road to Emery Down. Follow the road to the top of the hill overlooking Emery Down. The scattered houses of the village appear dotted along the hillside; their gardens making colourful oases among the dips and hollows. You pass a lane on the right in front of Honeysuckle Cottage called Silver Street.

Our road through the village turns left to pass the church and a group of almshouses built round a courtyard. They are all built of the same warm red brick. Christ Church, Emery Down, was built in 1864 from designs by William Butterfield. It was the gift of Admiral Boultbee who also endowed the almshouses which are known locally as 'Boultbee's cottages'.

Before the junction with the Bolderwood and Linwood road you pass the New Forest Inn. In the early 1700s a caravan stood on this site having claimed squatters' rights. Now the caravan forms the front lounge porchway and the Inn is built either side of it. Do not follow the Bolderwood road but bear right in front of the Inn following the unsignposted road leading to Stoney Cross. The village here is so pretty, its houses framed by Forest trees and encircled by buttercup-filled meadows, that it is easy to understand why it has always been popular with writers and artists. The novelist, Mary Braddon, lived nearby at Annesley in Bank. In 1862 her novel *Lady Audley's Secret* caused a sensation, selling nearly a million copies.

After about a quarter of a mile, just past a lane on the right, you will come to a turning on the left a few yards past a letter box. Turn left and when the track divides follow the right-hand track. The gravel finishes ahead of you but our way is right along a white path leading over the grass. Turn right and follow the path which brings you to the woods around the northern edge of James's Hill. Follow the path through the trees. When the path divides keep straight ahead down the left-hand path. As you cross a more open area a path joins our way from the right. Turn left along this path which at first is like a gully leading into the trees. You cross a grassy area as you approach Broom Hill Inclosure. The path divides and our way is straight ahead — the right hand of the two tracks. Now you follow a beautiful woodland path through old woods of oaks and beeches, holly and silver birches.

The first time I came this way the trees had all the fresh green of May. Dappled sunlight fell on glades of heather and bilberry bushes among a glorious tangle of russet bracken fronds. I was contemplating all this when a large fox came trotting round a curve in the path straight towards me. It would be difficult to say who was most surprised! He stopped, small triangular face alert, green eyes gleaming, red-brown body motionless. Then, with no sign of alarm or a moment's panic, he turned, his wide brush sweeping the path, and trotted round me to rejoin the path a few yards further on. There was no doubt in his mind who was the intruder.

This lovely path takes you all round the base of James's Hill which is on your left. There are very few hills like this in the Forest, isolated, over three hundred feet high and still retaining a thick gravel capping. The gravel made it valuable. On an old map of 1789 it is called 'gravel hill' and old diggings remain on the top. Until recent times all Forest roads were gravel. I am told that the main road from Ashurst through Lyndhurst was gravelled up to the beginning of the second world war. But in former days the less important pathways through the Forest were mud tracks. Coaches and carriages had to be preceded by armed postillions with a guide. At night large circular horn lanterns holding three candles each known as 'moons' were fixed to poles and attached to the stirrups of the postillions.

Ignore all side tracks until you come to a well-defined crossing path. Turn right to walk to a joining path in front of an open glade. Bear left along this path as it leads you towards the trees of Wood Crates. Now you can see our objective clearly, Acres Down, a high ridge of heath and gorse-covered moorland rising ahead, just a little to your right. Our way runs over the glade through the trees and across a valley to the ridge so, when the path divides at the edge of the glade, bear right over the glade, then follow the path into the trees. Cross a stream. When you see a glade ahead through the trees the path forks. Bear right again so that the high, smooth ridge of moorland is now directly ahead. Our way is clear, over the heath in the valley, then winding to the top of the ridge through low gorse and holly and silver birches. Climb to the top to find yourself in a wonderful place. You stand high in the heath at Acres Down. All around you spread billowing waves of woodlands. The dark pines of HighlandWater contrast with the bright greens of the oaks and beeches of Broom Hill and Wood Crates, James's and Lyndhurst Hills. There is a glimpse of Southampton, framed by these massed woods and far away on the horizon, the soft blue of the Isle of Wight hills. This is a place to rest the spirit.

Walk over the ridge along the main path over all minor cross tracks until you meet a broad, well-defined crosstrack where our main path turns right. Turn right and follow the path along the ridge with Highland Water valley and Inclosure on your left. After about a quarter of a mile the path dips slightly and you pass a gravel path on your right which leads back along the ridge. Ignore this and keep on until you see a pleasant green path on your right leading along a shallow valley over Pilmore Gate Heath. At this point, if you prefer the shorter walk, turn right and follow this path to meet the minor road from Emery Down that we followed at the beginning of our walk. At the road, turn right to walk back through the village.

To continue our longer walk, keep straight on past a Forestry Commission barrier to meet a crosstrack. Go over the crosstrack and follow the path as it bears left and walk down the hill through a wood to meet a lane beside Acres Down House and Farm. Look across the lane a little to your left and you will see a sign 'Acres Down House and Cottage only'. That is our way. Turn left past the sign and follow the track with the House and Cottage on your right. When the gravel ends keep straight on over the heath ahead.

A little to the left of our path a tall stand of pines shades an old marl pit. You will find these throughout the Forest where 'the right of marl' is still possessed by some Commoners. Marling was an ancient method of fertilising poor land by spreading over it material dug from pits like this. It was a skilled craft with a host of technical terms, songs, customs and sayings attached to it. Two sayings I have heard are 'he that marls moss shall have no loss' and 'he that marls clays flings all away'. Gangs of marlers went from farm to farm, one of whom was chosen as 'Lord of the Soil'. Passers-by were asked for money and at the end of the week there was a celebration at the local Inn. When a whole area was finished, everyone joined in — marlers, farmworkers, neighbours and tenants — there were drinks for all, songs, dancing and no doubt a good supper as well.

Our pleasant way winds over heathland dotted with trees, bearing slightly left towards a pine wood. When you reach the wood bear right along the track beside it, the wood on your left. The path bears a little away from the pines over the heath then steers you towards pine woods again. Here you meet a wide green crosstrack. The track leads left to a gate into the wood beside a trig point. We turn right and follow the main track as it leads over the heath with trees fairly close on the left. When the track divides follow the main track still as it bears right towards an old oak and beech wood. Our way is through the glades at the edge of the wood, shaded by some huge trees, the ground deep in mast.

We are heading towards the minor road from Stoney Cross to Emery Down. Just before you come to the road the track divides. Keep straight on (left track) towards a house ahead of you. You come to the road opposite this house, 'Ashers Top'. Cross the road and turn right and walk along the heath beside the road. Ignore the first bridleway sign you see pointing left and keep on for about a quarter of a mile in all until you come to another bridleway sign on the left. This is just past a letterbox and a lane leading to 'Tom's Corner'. Follow the path in the direction of the sign bearing left over the green. The path soon becomes a wide, deep lane leading down a fertile valley of small fields and fruit trees.

You are in the farming country which surrounds Minstead. I was intrigued by the old farm machines laid up on the grass beside the track. The path meets a lane at Newtown. Some thatched and half-timbered cottages here belie the truth of the name! Turn right along the lane for a few yards to a 'phone box on the corner, then right again. The lane brings you quickly back to the minor road again, the one from Stoney Cross to Emery Down.

Cross the road and immediately opposite is a lane leading downhill. Follow the lane, cross the stream, Bartley Water, and up the road to rejoin our earlier route at Acres Down House. It is the sunken lane climbing uphill on your left if you stand on the road with Acres Down House on your right. When the track levels and bears a little left turn right — past the Forestry Commission barrier which is not visible at first — along the path we followed earlier in our walk. Turn left along the green path I mentioned as a quick way back for the shorter walk. It is the first path you meet on your left. This lovely way rambles along the valley past a little pond. The path becomes a wide gravelled track which leads you back to the minor road just above Emery Down.

Turn right and walk back through the village to Swan Green. The car park is on your right or you can catch the bus back to Southampton on the main A35 road opposite.

Walk 5

GRITNAM AND THE GREAT WOODS OF LYNDHURST

Starting point: Swan Green car park, near Lyndhurst. Bus: Swan Green, near Lyndhurst.

Distance: 4 miles.

This walk takes us through the great oak and beech woods that surround the Forest capital, Lyndhurst. As we walk, I will describe some of the people you would once have met there making a living in these ancient woods. Today, of course, some Forest homes still retain their rights of common, entitling their occupants to graze their animals and gather fuel in the Forest. But not so long ago, the Forest was the home of the gypsies and other folk whose livelihoods welded them firmly to the area: swineherds, adder-catchers and charcoal burners. Many of the tracks we follow through these great woods were made by them.

We start from Swan Green, a small hamlet close to Lyndhurst beside the A35 road to Bournemouth. The Bournemouth bus stops here or, as it is so close, you can walk from Lyndhurst. If you are coming by car from Southampton, turn right off the A35 at Swan Green, in the direction of Emery Down. After about a hundred yards turn into Swan Green car park on your left. Between the car park and the A35 is a wide green used as a cricket pitch. Our footpath climbs through the trees on the opposite side of the green from the car park from a point close to the main road. From the car park, walk diagonally downhill across the green towards the rails which border the A35, heading for the corner by the road where the rails meet the wooded slopes of Lyndhurst Hill. Just before you reach the rails you will see our path climbing through the trees running roughly parallel with the main road.

If you arrive at Swan Green by bus, walk beside the main road in the direction

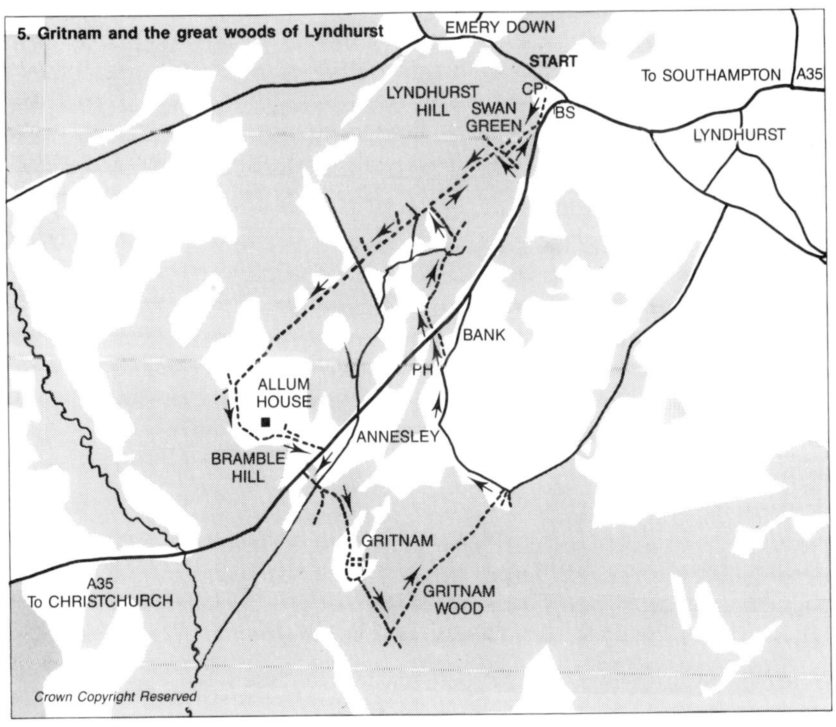

of Bournemouth for a few yards. Go through the gate at the edge of the green on your right to our path leading immediately uphill on the left.

Follow this narrow woodland path as it climbs through oaks, beeches and hollies with the A35 on your left. After a short distance you come to a wide crossing track. Turn right and follow this way for only a few yards until you come to a green crosstrack. Turn left here near the top of Lyndhurst Hill and now a beautiful wide path lies before you. This lovely woodland walk winds downhill beneath arches of spreading boughs with occasional glimpses of soft Forest lawns on either side. As we came down the hill a dainty roe deer skipped across our path to stand motionless in the shadow of the trees watching us pass. Cross two streams to more open heathland. Keep straight on over all crossing tracks and small areas of heath until our way is bordered by part of the walled garden of Allum House.

Allum House is typical of the family homes built or acquired by wealthy business or professional men after the coming of the railway in the mid-nineteenth century made the Forest more accessible. The Forest provided the seclusion and sporting facilities such homes required without the need of maintaining an estate. This pleasant house was once the home of the Fenwick family, who donated the hospital which bears their name to Lyndhurst in 1908.

The wall is beautifully built of warm red brick and our way follows its curve left round the building then to meet a gravel track. The track curves left in front of Allum House then right over Allum Green. Follow the track to the main road, the A35. Cross the cattle grid, turn right and walk beside the road for about a hundred yards. Look for a narrow path leading to a gate on the left. Cross the road, go through the gate and a wide gravel path leads you over a stream and into the oak and beech-shaded glades of Gritnam wood. Leave the gravel track as it curves right and keep straight on for a short way until you see glimpses of cottages through the trees ahead. This is Gritnam, a compact Forest hamlet, completely encircled by ancient woods.

Gritnam has remained without any tendency to straggle into the surrounding woods. Evidently the people who live there have always liked it that way for I came across a revealing story in *It Happened in Hampshire*. An old cottager recalls her grandmother telling her that one day a queen (she wasn't certain which one) was riding past Gritnam and tore her dress. Her grandmother mended the tear and the queen gave permission for her family to take in from the Forest as much ground as they could dig within a certain specified time. No one did any digging, the permission lapsed and Gritnam had no additions made to its boundaries!

Bear a little right towards the cottages and follow the road round the hamlet, the houses on your left. Just past some white cottages the road round the villages turns sharply left. Before this turn, directly in front of the cottages, take the green path that leads right, past a barrier into the heart of the woods. Walk down the hill to a green crosstrack and then turn left in the direction of Bank.

As we walked beneath magnificent oaks swathed to their upper boughs in holly and through groves of silver-grey beeches our feet crunched through thick layers of acorns and beech mast, or seed. This is still grazed today by pigs during the Pannage Season but it was once the Forest's most valuable harvest. In the *Domesday Book*, the worth of Forest holdings was assessed by the number of pigs their crop of mast could support. William Gilpin, vicar of Boldre, touring the Forest at the beginning of the nineteenth century, writes in great detail about the swineherd's task, particularly his slow and careful method of introducing the animals to the Forest.

Gilpin writes, 'The method of treating hogs at this season of migration, and of reducing a large herd of these unmanageable brutes to perfect obedience and good government, is curious. The first step the swine-herd takes is to investigate some close sheltered part of the forest, where there is a conveniency of water; and plenty of oak, or beech mast . . . he fixes next on some spreading tree, round the bole of which he wattles a slight, circular fence . . . covering it roughly with boughs and sods, he fills it plentifully with straw or fern.' He then gets together his herd of five or six hundred pigs, then 'having driven them to their destined habitation, he gives them a plentiful supper of acorns or beech mast sounding his horn during the repast. He then turns them into the litter where, after a long journey and a hearty meal, they sleep deliciously.' The swine-herd watches them for three days then 'he leaves them a little more to themselves, having an eye however on their evening hours. But as their bellies are full, they seldom wander far from home, retiring commonly, very orderly to bed.' After this, he throws the sty open leaving his well-behaved animals to cater for themselves.

The pannage season when pigs may be turned out by the Commoners into the Forest begins in September, when the acorns and beech mast have fallen. Ponies nibble these also and, as too much is bad for them, the pigs perform a useful service as well as enjoying what must be the highlight of their year.

C J Cornish, writing about the Forest in 1894, tells about other people who made a living in these great woods, the charcoal burners. 'In a centre of a clearing,' he writes, 'surrounded on three sides by a towering ring of monster beeches, was a deserted charcoal burner's hut, with a burning circle in front of the door. The hut looks like a large ant hill covered with scales of turf turned grass inwards, with a kind of mushroom cup on the apex and a square door and porch hewn of roughly squared oak. A glimpse of the interior shows that the framework is a cone of strong oak poles, and the only furniture a couple of sacks of dry beech leaves, a low wooden bench, and one or two iron pots.'

Charcoal burning was an important Forest industry. Charcoal was used to smelt iron until the use of coke became general and was an ingredient in the manufacture of gunpowder. A large gunpowder works flourished in the Forest at Eyeworth near Fritham until 1910. The making of charcoal was a slow and skilled occupation demanding the careful exclusion of air throughout the whole burning process so the men lived in the Forest in wigwam-shaped huts of branches and turf beside their 'hearths' where the wood was burnt. Mr Bill Veal of Emery Down recalls that his grandfather 'Old Marky' Veal used to supply charcoal for the use of Queen Victoria at Osborne House on the Isle of Wight. There was a temporary revival of the industry during the 1914–18 War.

Cornish tells too of another, much stranger occupation. 'A similar hut' he writes, 'in Gritnam wood is inhabited throughout the year by an adder hunter. He lives in health and comfort with a low oak bench for his bed, and a faggot of heather for curtain and door.' Adder fat was much valued for medicinal purposes and adder hunting was a profitable business.

Follow the path towards Bank to an open clearing on the brow of a hill where our way becomes indistinct. Walk straight over the clearing and through the trees ahead to the minor road that runs from Lyndhurst — ahead of us — through the little village of Bank to meet the A35 at a point just south of Lyndhurst Hill. Turn left and follow the road. You look over a huddle of red-roofed cottages to the shallow valley through which the A35 runs to Lyndhurst. Far right, on the hill top, rises the spire of Lyndhurst church and beyond the road ahead is the steep slope of Lyndhurst Hill. Walk down the road through the village, bearing right past a cottage dated 1600 and up the lane in front. When you come to the Royal Oak Inn on your left, turn right onto the road leading to the A35. Follow this lane for only a few yards — look carefully for a copse on the left. Beside the copse, a narrow path runs downhill to the road. Follow this path, copse on the right, to a gate by the A35. (If you miss this path, follow the lane to the main road, then turn left and walk the few yards to the gate.) Cross the main road, turn left, and a few yards further on you will see a gate into the Forest on your right. Go through the gate and walk straight ahead through a fringe of trees to a wide green lawn. We are aiming to join our original path from Swan Green to Allum House which runs along the hillside immediately opposite.

The path that used to run from the gate we have just entered, across the green, over a stream and up the hillside to meet our original path, is no longer visible but another path does follow much the same route a little further north. To pick up this path needs careful navigation for about 150 yards as there is no clear way. Turn right when you come to the green lawn and walk straight ahead, hugging the fringe of trees, with the open green on your left and the A35 through the trees on your right. After about a hundred yards small thickets of trees spread over to your left. Keep straight on between the trees. (On your left is a small wood, then the open green.) After about fifty yards you come to an open space and in the middle a little to your left, you will see a concrete bridge over a tiny stream. You are now back on a good path again! Cross the concrete bridge and follow the path as it takes you over the grass ahead and then turns sharply left uphill. This brings you quickly back to our original beautiful path from Swan Green. Turn right and retrace your steps uphill. When you reach the crossing track turn right for just a short way, then left to follow the narrow path back to the cricket field. Go through the gate in the corner to the bus stop, or cross diagonally back to Swan Green car park.

· ASHURST ·

Ashurst is a pleasantly leafy village on the border of the Forest, only seven miles from Southampton. It tends to be overlooked by walkers but it is the gateway to some of the most beautiful areas in the north-east of the Forest.

You will find ample parking in the public car park close to Ashurst Hospital and the village is only twenty minutes from Southampton by train. The station is called Lyndhurst Road. Ashurst has excellent restaurants and inns and a large campsite nearby.

Walk 6

BORDER COUNTRY: CHURCHPLACE AND THE NORTH-EAST TERRACES

Starting point: Ashurst car park, close to Ashurst Hospital. Bus: Ashurst Hospital. Train: Lyndhurst Road (Ashurst)

Distance: Eight miles all round. Optional shorter route about three miles.

Campsite: Ashurst. Turn right from the entrance for Ashurst Hospital and car park close by.

Border country is always fascinating. This walk takes you along the north-east boundary of the Forest where there is an almost startling contrast between the Forest, so much a world of its own, and the farming land it adjoins. The land is high, and looking over the Forest from paths that sometimes follow terraces along the hillsides, you see wave after wave of woodland rolling westward in every imaginable shade of green.

Allow at least four hours for this walk, a little over eight miles round. If you can spare a full day you will be able to allow yourself more 'time to stand and stare'. But I also suggest an optional shorter route of about three miles. The starting point is Ashurst village, Lyndhurst Road Station if you arrive by train.

We begin from the village car park. If you are driving from Southampton turn left before the railway bridge and you will see the park just past Ashurst Hospital

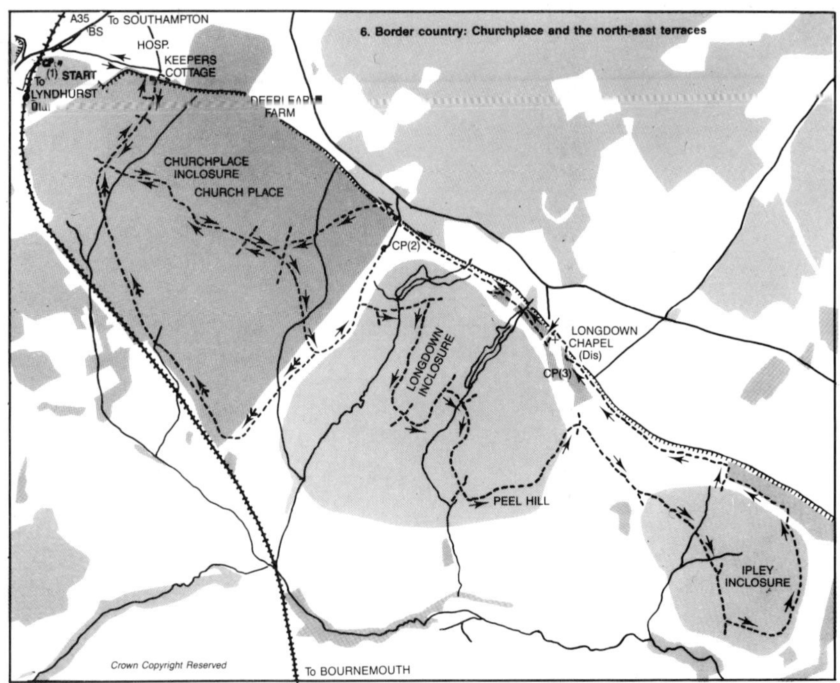

Additions to Key:

Sta   *Lyndhurst Road Station (Ashurst)*   CP(3) *Longdown car park*
CP(1) *Ashurst car park*
CP(2) *Deerleap car park*   *For general Key see p. viii*

---

gates. From the station, turn right and cross the bridge, then right again into the car park. If you are camping at Ashurst, turn right from the campsite entrance, cross the bridge, then right again for the car park.

Stand with your back to the car park and the Hospital on your right, and you will see a wide gravel track running behind the Hospital towards Churchplace Inclosure. This is our way.

The white buildings of the Hospital were once the New Forest Union workhouse. As you follow the track towards the cricket ground you will notice some fine trees, survivors of what were once dense woods fringing a forest lawn. The lawn stretched beside the Southampton road for two miles. One of the first writers to describe the Forest, William Gilpin, noted in 1790: 'The name of this beautiful and extensive forest scene is Hounsdown; so named probably from the fair advantage it gives the hound in pursuit. If he can drive his chase, from the thickets into this open plain, it is probable he will there secure him.' This area is still called Hounsdown today and nearby is Hunter's Inn hill.

Follow the track past a notice 'Churchplace Cottage only' until you come to this attractive forest lodge on your right. Turn right through a gate into Churchplace Inclosure.

The keeper's house was built the same time as the woods were planted — 1810 — as an inscription over a window of the cottage indicates. Squirrels revel in these woods of young oaks and beeches. They scamper across your path rustling the dead leaves, skim up the tree trunks to pause spreadeagled if they suspect you have seen them, and leap from branch to branch above your head. Look for woodpeckers too, particular the brilliantly coloured large green bird with his strange 'laughing' call.

Keep to the gravel track until you come to a crosstrack where another gravel path joins our way on the left. Turn left here. The track rises a little and then bears right past a knoll crowned with much older beeches on your left. This is Churchplace, possibly the site of one of the Saxon churches William the Conqueror was said to have destroyed when he declared the New Forest his exclusive hunting reserve in 1079.

The name suggests this could have been the site of a church of course, and if you explore the top you will find some interesting embankments. But was William such a villain as the Saxon chroniclers claim? According to the Winchester chronicle 'Through the space of thirty miles, the whole county, which was fruitful in a high degree, was laid waste. The churches, gardens, and houses were all destroyed, and the whole reduced by the king's order into a chase for beasts.' As many as thirty-six parish churches are said to have been destroyed. Later historians question this. And that most warmhearted and outspoken of Hampshire travellers, William Cobbett, remarked as he rode through the Forest in 1823 that the area could never have been rich or populous — the soil was too poor. He pointed out that as in the original area of the Forest there still remain eleven parish churches on sites where churches were in existence before the time of the Conqueror, 'if he destroyed thirty six parish churches, what a populous county this must have been! There must have been forty seven parish churches over the whole district — one parish church to every four and three quarter square miles.' Have a look at this strange hill, and see what you think!

Follow the track as it bears right to a cross path. Now keep straight ahead down the gravel track opposite. Dark pines cast heavy shade over your path. On the right is Deerleap Inclosure. Gilpin explains this Forest name: 'Here a stag was once shot; which in the agony of death, collecting his force, gave a bound, which astonished those who saw it. It was immediately commemorated by two posts, which were fixed at the two extremities of the leap, where they still remain. The space between them is somewhat more than eighteen yards.'

You soon come to another crosstrack. Leave the gravel and keep straight on down the green ride ahead. Now you are really in the still heart of the pinewoods, walking on a delicious soft and scented carpet of emerald moss. Walk down to a bridge over a tiny tributary of the Beaulieu river then up the opposite slope to a gate. Go through the gate into a different world! You are now standing on the open windswept heath dotted with gnarled Scots pines. (For the shorter walk, about three miles round, turn right to the bridge over the railway. Just before the bridge, turn right again and return at first close to the line, then keeping to the same track, through Churchplace Inclosure.)

To continue on our present route, cross the heath towards Longdown Inclosure. Ignore the tempting gate into the Inclosure directly ahead, and turn left and walk on for about a quarter of a mile with the Inclosure on your right to the next large gate into the Inclosure. Turn right through this gate into Longdown. Ignore the first track on the right and follow the path ahead. These are new woods, planted in the 1960s. After crossing a stream the path climbs a little. Take the first track on the right now. This hugs the hillside so that you follow a wide terrace with a valley rippling with young pines beside you. The path bears left. Go straight over a crosstrack keeping to the main path as it bears more left to a gravel road. For the next quarter of a mile we follow wide gravel roads but then we are back to quiet Forest paths again. You come to a joining gravel track on the right. Turn right and follow it downhill. When the track divides, keep straight on (right-hand path). Our way now becomes a green ride and bears right to bring us towards Peel Hill. Go straight over a crosstrack, keeping to the main ride as it bears left to bring us to the eastern edge of Longdown Inclosure.

Go through the gate onto the heath. You are now in a wonderful part of the Forest with a magnificent view west, over the woods and heath each side of the Beaulieu river, across the great trees of Matley to Lyndhurst church spire against the skyline. From the gate walk a few yards to a crossing path. Do not follow this but look across it to a path which winds ahead a little to your right. It crosses the heath in the direction of a dark cluster of Scots pines. Go over the crossing track and follow this path over the heath. The moor dips away from you to give glorious views and I think you will agree that this is one of the most lovely places in the whole Forest. As you approach the wood, the path divides. Keep straight on (left-hand path) over smooth green lawns under the pines to the gate leading into the wood.

This is an ideal spot for a rest and a snack. Just visible through the trees on the left is a track which leads through Marchwood to Cracknore Hard on Southampton Water. Tales are told in *It Happened in Hampshire* of smugglers who landed at Cracknore, loaded their contraband onto horses with shoes reversed and led them over this heath to a house near the present Beaulieu Road Station. When houses have been rebuilt, several 'hides' have been found, some even containing rotting casks. Ipley Manor, just south of the wood, was a known sanctuary for smugglers. As late as 1873 a smuggler was caught red-handed with his cargo off Cracknore.

Walk through the gate into Ipley Wood. This is also newly planted. When you come to a T-junction turn right. Keep straight on past a joining track on the left to a gate at the southern edge of the Inclosure. Here is another place to pause and look over the heath far over the woods that fringe the Beaulieu river. Do not go through the gate but follow the track left which swings round in a semi-circle to bring you to a gate at the north-east edge of Ipley Inclosure. Here we turn for home. Our return route is a direct one, following the Forest boundary along the edge of Ipley and Longdown Inclosures, keeping the trees on our left.

Go through the gate and turn left along the green path parallel with the Forest Boundary. This boundary area is a kind of no-man's-land of green lawns alive with rabbits. It's interesting to compare the long line of dark Forest trees on the left with the farming land on the right dotted with neat houses beside tidily hedged fields. When you come to a crosstrack with a path leading left into the wood, turn right for just a few yards, then left along a path to the left of a fence — heading as before — to cross a plank bridge. Keep straight on uphill along the green path over the heath with the Forest boundary on your right. Ahead, you will see the dark line of the pines marking the eastern edge of Longdown Inclosure. The path now winds close to the boundary fence on your right and meets a lane. Keep straight on over the heath with the lane close on your right or walk down the lane. At the edge of the Inclosure you come to Longdown car park. Join the lane here if you have not already done so, at the car park entrance. A few yards further down the lane past the car park you will see Longdown Chapel — still recognizable as such although it is now a private house. Follow the lane to the chapel and just beyond it turn left along a gravel track towards a gate into the Inclosure. Do not go through the gate but turn right just before it and walk down the heath with the Inclosure on your left to pick up a good gravel track leading ahead downhill over a stream. Follow this over an open area. The gravel ends and the path divides. Take the narrow, right-hand path that climbs a little through the gorse bushes. This leads you over a hill and becomes a pleasant little path leading you over a stream and on over the heath towards Deerleap Inclosure.

Here our way is interrupted by Deerleap Car Park. Walk straight across the park to the point where a lane leads right to join the road. Our way is the broad green track you see straight ahead. It is barred to prevent motor access, but it is a simple matter for us to cross the cattle grid and pick our way left to join it. Now for a little careful navigation! Follow this wide way for about a hundred yards and just before the top of a slight rise look for a gate on your left leading into Deerleap Inclosure. Turn left through the gate into the Inclosure to walk along a soft turf path bordered with Scots pines. Keep straight on over a gravel crosstrack. When you come to the next gravel crosstrack turn right and follow this way quickly back to Churchplace. We are now on the track we followed at the beginning of our walk. When you reach the fourways again, turn right to make your way to the keeper's cottage. Go through the gate, then left to see Ashurst Hospital and Lyndhurst Road Station a short distance ahead.

Walk 7

ASHURST AND MATLEY WOOD

Starting point: Ashurst car park, close to Ashurst Hospital. Bus: Ashurst Hospital. Train: Lyndhurst Road (Ashurst).

Distance: 6 miles.

Campsite: Ashurst. Turn right from the entrance for Ashurst Hospital and car park close by.

This walk from Ashurst, although only six miles round, takes us through pine woods across open heaths to one of the oldest oak woods in the Forest, Matley Wood. We return through continuous woodlands with trees of all kinds — oak, beech, ash, sweet chestnut, rowan, silver birch and pine predominating.

Our starting point is Ashurst car park. The car park is in front of the main gates of the hospital, just off the A35, to the right of a small row of shops. Driving from Southampton, turn left immediately before the bridge that crosses the railway from Southampton to Bournemouth. You can, of course, come to Ashurst on the train to start this walk. The station is called Lyndhurst Road. From the platform, turn right over the bridge to the car park. Buses stop close by and there is also a

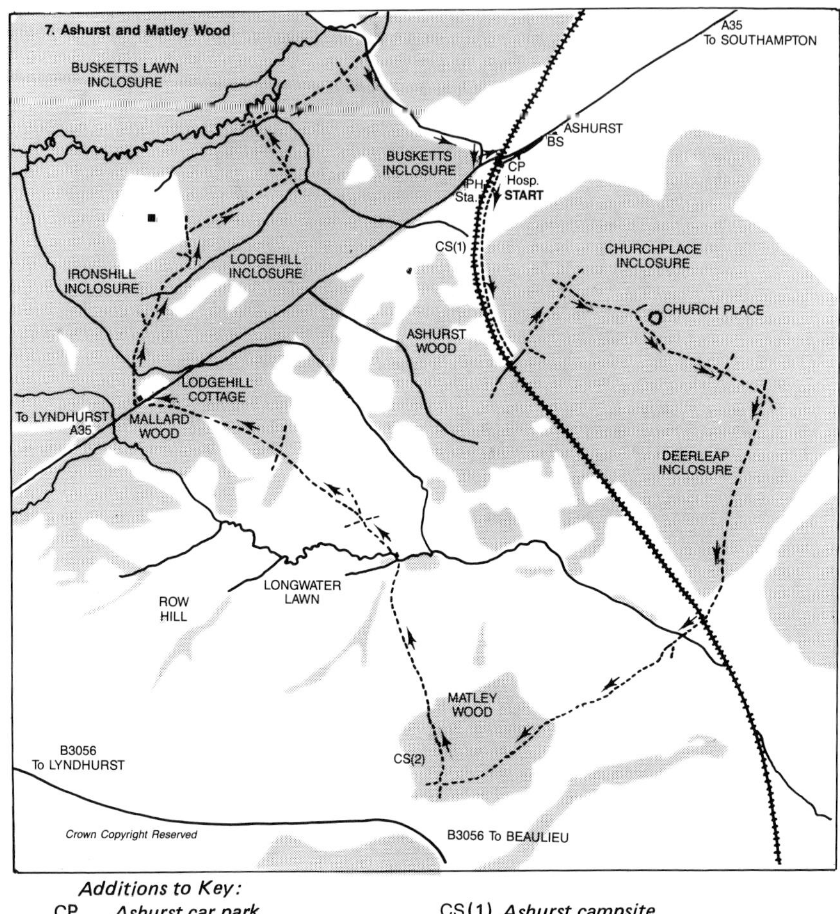

convenient campsite.

From the car park turn left along the lane towards the railway line, then turn left through the gate which leads you on to the wide lawns beside the railway. Follow the path with the edge of Churchplace Inclosure on your left and the railway to your right. Go through the next gate where a track leads right over a railway bridge. Our way is left, into Churchplace Inclosure.

When you come to a gravel track bear left for just a few steps then follow the track straight ahead. This quickly brings you to a crossways (greenway on the left). Follow the gravel track right as it climbs gently uphill towards Churchplace itself. Our path runs to the right of Churchplace, a knoll crowned with oaks and beeches.

There are several 'Churchplaces' in the Forest and this, I think, is the most interesting. They present a mystery which, like the death of William Rufus, is still not fully explained. No love was lost between the Saxon chroniclers and William the Conqueror. When he declared this part of southern England his New Forest they recorded, with appropriate venom, his destruction of villages. Even worse, because it was sacrilege, was his alleged removal of churches. Accounts in the chronicles vary but between twenty and forty churches are supposed to have been destroyed. Are the 'Churchplaces' dotted about the Forest the sites of some of these Saxon churches? Certainly the knoll we see would have made an ideal site. The chroniclers themselves are confused about the numbers and as William Cobbett argued, it is hard to imagine that the arid soil of the Forest could ever have supported sufficient people to require so many churches. The mystery remains. I explored Churchplace and discovered some curious ridges and rounded embankments. Could they have been the foundations of a destroyed Saxon church?

Continue along the gravel track over a crosstrack into Deerleap Inclosure. When you come to the next crosstrack, turn right and follow the gravel track downhill towards the railway line. Just before our path turns sharply right, look for a gate leading to open heathland on your left. Go through the gate, turn right, and cross the bridge over the railway.

At the other side of the line, the path leads over a stream — a very young Beaulieu river. A few yards after the stream our path divides; keep to the right-hand track. Our way now winds through the heather of the open heath towards the line of Matley Wood directly ahead, one of the most beautiful oak woods in the Forest. Walk through the outlying fringe of silver birches into the soft green glades beneath these fine old trees. All sorts of wildlife love Matley. It is the home of deer, badgers, foxes, squirrels of course, and the smallest and rarest of the woodpecker family, the lesser spotted woodpecker. Every glade is rich with woodland flowers and ferns.

Follow the main path right through Matley until you see ahead a barrier leading to a car park. About thirty yards before you come to the barrier a track leads right downhill through the trees to the northern edge of Matley Wood. This is our way but the track is very faint at first. Look for a large whitened fallen tree beside a huge stump. Turn right past the tree and walk straight ahead and the track soon becomes clear. When you come to the fringe of the wood a well-defined path leads straight ahead through some gorse, then out on to the open heath.

As we walked over this moor, lapwings circled our heads, calling their plaintive cries. The path leads down to a bridge over the Beaulieu river. We had crossed the bridge and, pausing to look back at the stream, we saw what looked like a branch sticking up out of the water. When it moved we realised it was a heron. Once these great birds were common in the Forest and there was a famous heronry at nearby Vinney Ridge. The heron rose above the water, flapping its heavy wings in a slow, lazy fashion, but we went no closer. There was a chance it could have been nesting, but more likely it had only been standing in the shallows enjoying a meal of fish and frogs.

After you have crossed the stream another heath opens before you. Follow the path straight over the heath towards Mallard Wood — from the bridge our path bears a little left. About half way over the heath go over a crossing track. When the path divides, follow the left-hand track in the direction of the nearest trees. Keep straight on over another crosstrack to enter Mallard Wood. This is another lovely 'ancient and ornamental' woodland with some particularly fine unpollarded beech trees. Cross a little heath to walk through the most northerly part of Mallard Wood. Go straight over all crosstracks and soon you will see the main A35 road ahead. Before you come to the road the path bears left to a gate and stile beside the road.

On the other side of the road, a little to your left, you will see a keeper's cottage. Cross the road and go through the gate beside the cottage into Lodgehill Inclosure. A few yards further on, bear right along a gravelled track. When you come to a crossways go straight across following the track immediately ahead with Ironshill Inclosure on your left.

This name has an interesting story to tell, a story which takes us back a thousand years before the Normans, perhaps even to pre-Roman times. East Hampshire was always rich in iron ore and in early days the ore was brought to the New Forest, where there was a plentiful source of charcoal, to be smelted. The name 'Ironshill' occurs in other parts of the Forest also. High ground was essential to enable the wind to fan the tall cylindrical furnaces in which the iron-ore was packed between layers of charcoal. From the coins and pottery which have been found in cinder heaps, these foundries were working in Roman times. Later much more elaborate smelting works were built in the valleys using water power to drive huge hammers like the one at Sowley Pond, near Beaulieu, whose thudding became a characteristic sound of the New Forest.

Cross the private drive to Ironshill Lodge, and a few yards further on turn right. You are now heading due east for Ashurst with the A35 through the trees on your right. Follow the gravel track as it bears round to the left, past two joining tracks on the right and one on the left. Walk on and take the next right turn, following the gravel track, just before a stream with a footbridge. This brings you to a gate leading to the minor road which runs from Ashurst through Woodlands village to Cadnam. From the gate turn right and follow the road as it bears right, uphill, to meet the A35 just before the railway bridge. Lyndhurst Road Station is immediately opposite. Cross the bridge and turn right for Ashurst car park.

· BROCKENHURST ·

Brockenhurst is many people's favourite Forest village. Like all Forest villages, it spreads itself in a comfortable fashion over heaths and round green lawns. Wander down any of the little lanes that apparently lead nowhere and you will come across scenes that seem untouched by time: clusters of old cottages covered in vines and roses defended by immensely thick hedges from the ponies and donkeys grazing nearby, a stream shaded by enormous trees whose roots entwined along the bank shelter the first primroses, and alone, on its hill overlooking the Forest, a church older than the *Domesday Book*.

Brockenhurst is easily reached by bus and train and makes an ideal centre for a Forest holiday. There is a large campsite close by at Hollands Wood.

Walk 8

BROCKENHURST VILLAGE RAMBLE

Starting point: Brockenhurst central car park off Brookley Road, opposite the Post Office. Bus and train: Brockenhurst.

Distance: About two miles.

Campsite: Hollands Wood, near Brockenhurst.

Forest villages tend to tuck their treasures away — you must leave the main streets to discover them. This short ramble reveals some of Brockenhurst's hidden gems.

From the central car park in Brockenhurst, off Brookley Road, return to the main street, turn right and walk down to the watersplash. Cross the bridge and turn left along the minor road. Cross the end of 'The Rise' and you will see a fence on your left round the last house before a green Forest lawn. Leave the road and turn left over the lawn. This is Culverley — the 'dove's meadow'. Cross over a small bridge and follow the path past the school on your left. This brings you to the B3055. Cross the road, turn left and walk along the road for only a few yards. Look for a footpath sign pointing right. Turn right at the sign and follow a narrow path to cross the end of a Close. Straight ahead you will see a gate leading to a footbridge over the railway. Cross the bridge and go through a gate immediately ahead which leads you to a lovely path through a meadow shaded by old oaks.

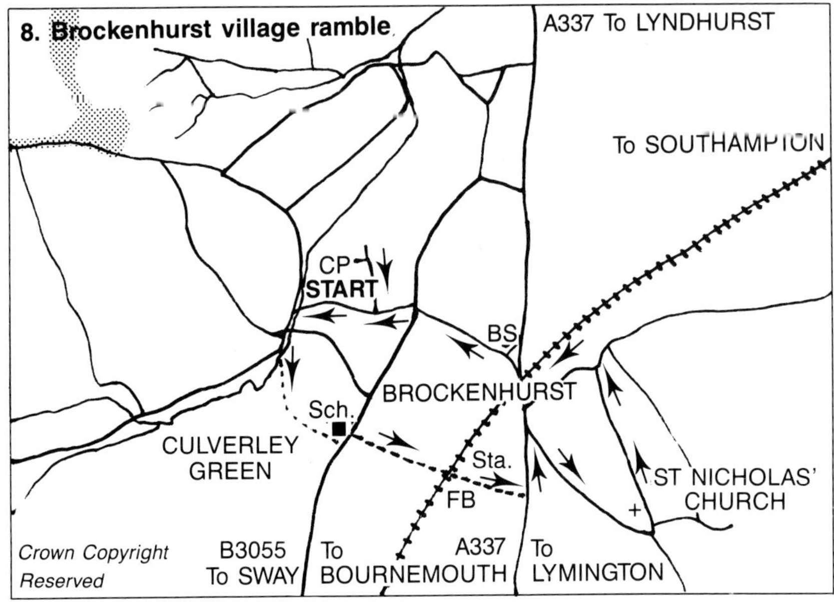

Additions to Key:
Sch   *School*
Sta   *Brockenhurst Station*
CP   *Brockenhurst car park*

For general Key see p. viii

The path runs high along the side of hollows and embankments dense with thickets of wild roses. Cross a stile to a main road, the A337. Turn left and walk beside the road for about fifty yards to a lane on your right with a sign to St Nicholas' Church.

Walk up the lane to the church which stands on a hill above the village. First impressions of a tower glimpsed behind an enormous yew could be rather sombre but as the lane bears a little left to come round the south front of the church you face a little stone building full of homely charm.

There has been a church here since Saxon times — there is some Saxon herring-bone masonry in the walls — and the present building is mentioned in the *Domesday Book*. There is a mass-clock carved beside the south doorway which worked like a sundial to indicate the time for mass. The doorway's chevron mouldings show Norman architecture at its best. The church is open for Sunday services and on weekday afternoons between May and September. There is more fine Norman work inside and a curtained 'Squire's Pew'. Close to the pew is a picture of Harry 'Brusher' Mills, a handsome bearded gentleman who has become part of Forest lore. He lived in a hut in the woods and caught snakes, much valued for their uses in medicine. His grave is in the churchyard near the New Zealand cemetery on the east side of the central level. More than a hundred New Zealand, Indian and other soldiers died in the base hospital at Brockenhurst during the First World War. The Imperial War Graves Commission ordered the replacement of the original wooden crosses with engraved headstones and erected a memorial. Each year a service is held in their memory on the Sunday next to Anzac Day.

Leave the lane as it turns right and bear left down a track that drops downhill beside the church like a long green tunnel. This brings you to a minor road. Turn left and walk back to the A337, almost opposite the Station. Turn right over the level crossing. Bear left past the island in the road to walk down Brookley Road. Keep straight on over the crossroads and you will see the car park on your right.

Walk 9

BROCKENHURST RIVER AND NORTH WEIRS

Starting point: Brockenhurst central car park off Brookley Road, opposite the Post Office. Bus and train: Brockenhurst.

Distance: 5 miles.

Campsite: Hollands Wood.

Brockenhurst means 'the badger's wood'. Badgers are particular about where they live. They like old woods with great trees whose roots have worked the earth soft so they can excavate their burrows or setts easily and they insist on a plentiful supply of drinking water. Brockenhurst fulfills these conditions perfectly. The village lies among glorious old woodlands and is interlaced with streams. North of the village runs the river which flows into the Solent at Lymington. If, like the badger, you enjoy old woods and streams then this walk is a 'must'.

From the central car park turn right to walk down to the watersplash. Turn right here and follow the white railings by the stream. When these end look for some small bridges on your right leading over the stream to the houses. Look carefully just by the third bridge and you will see a small wooden gate opening to a narrow streamside footpath. Follow this path as it leads you along the bank. You are in the heart of the village — gardens border the river — but this is a real Forest stream with trees spreading twisting coils of roots around its banks and ferns dimly reflected in its reddish-brown water.

Aother small gate leads you to a lane. Turn left and follow the stream for a short distance to a road near a 'phone box. Bear left along the road for a few yards until you see an 'Access to Allotments' sign on your left. Leave the road here but do not follow the track to the allotments. Instead, bear right along a path beside a little stream, keeping the stream on your right. Beyond the stream, the houses look over the wide heath you are crossing which is called Butts Lawn. This is named after the Butts, or targets, set here for archery practise in the days when every young villager was bound by law to practise using the long bow. Only practise from boyhood could ensure muscles sufficiently strong to bend the deadly yew bows which wrought such havoc at Agincourt and Crècy. Look ahead and you will see a long line of trees which mark the borders of the river. Our path bears a little left over another small stream and now leads directly towards the line of woodland. When you reach the edge of the woods, follow the path left for a short distance with the woodland on your right. When you come to a little path leading right, turn right to follow it through the trees, over a small bridge, to the banks

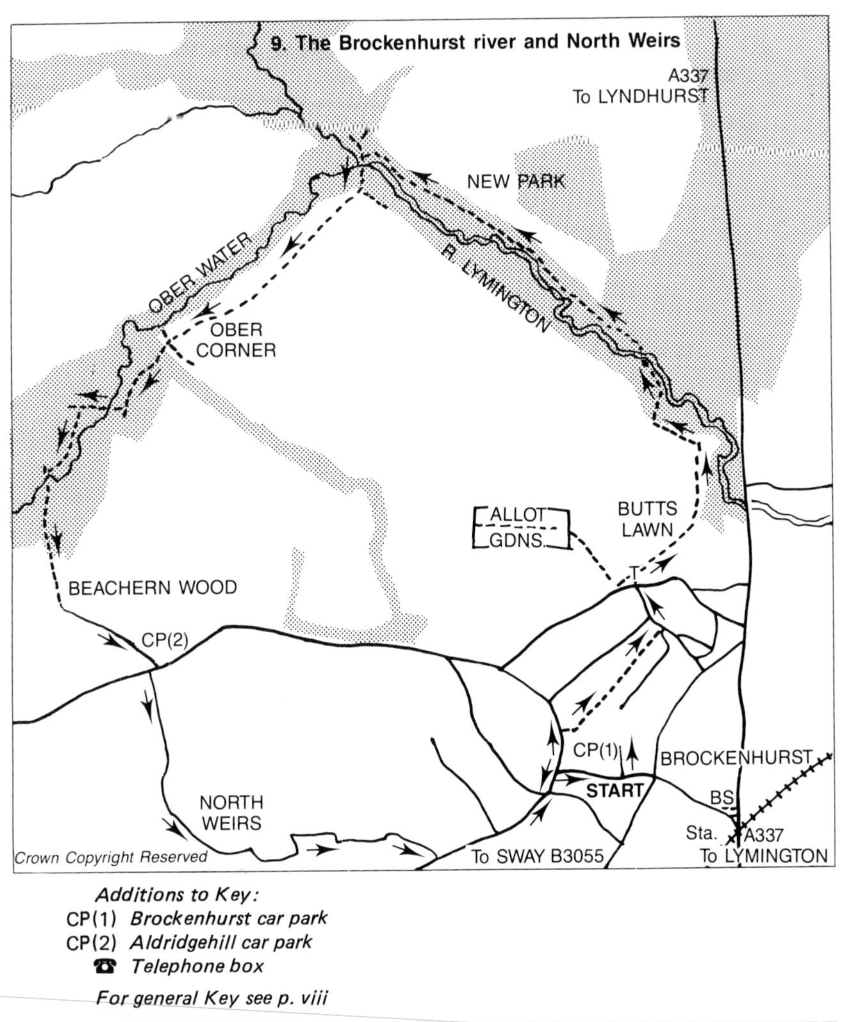

Additions to Key:
CP(1) *Brockenhurst car park*
CP(2) *Aldridgehill car park*
☎ *Telephone box*

For general Key see p. viii

of the river. Bear left along the river bank to a bridge. Cross over the bridge, turn left and walk on beside the river.

This is a beautiful woodland walk. Sometimes you are close to the river as it runs dark beneath the oaks and beeches and sometimes further away walking over grassy lawns dotted with tangles of brambles, honeysuckle and wild roses. Close on your right you will see the fields of New Park. New Park Manor was Charles II's favourite hunting lodge. He created this field system of some two hundred and forty acres in 1670 as a royal deer park to replace the ancient inclosure south-east of Lyndhurst. Each year the New Forest Show is held here on the last Wednesday and Thursday of July.

Follow the path beside the river until you come to a large wooden bridge, Bolderford Bridge. Here a small stream, Ober Water, flows into the river and this little stream will now be our guide. Turn left over the bridge and walk through a narrow belt of woodland to the open heath. Turn right here along a wide gravel track. It is more pleasant to walk on the heath or by the streamside in line with the track. When you come to the crossroads at Ober Corner, keep straight on along the metalled road ahead. Look for a bridge over the Ober Water stream on your right. Cross over the bridge and turn left to follow the bank. Soon you come to a wide path leading you through more beautiful woodland along the streamside. When you come to the next wooden footbridge you will see the red marked posts that indicate the Ober Water Forestry Commission trail. Turn left over the footbridge but do not follow the trail markings. Instead keep straight on along a pleasant path fringed with pines which, to judge by its name, Beachern Wood, was once a beech wood. The path leads to a metalled road. Keep straight on through Aldridgehill car park to a wider metalled road.

Over the road you will see a stony track with a 'Please drive slowly' sign. Cross the road and follow this track past Ober House and the scattering of houses that are North Weirs on your left. Over to your right you have beautiful views over White Moor to the woods of Hincheslea. As you walk you will notice that although the houses you pass are all different they are in perfect harmony with the Forest. Follow the track as it bears left round North Weirs to meet the Brockenhurst–Burley road. Turn left and walk back to the watersplash at the foot of Brookley Road. A quieter alternative to the road is to cross over to the right of the road and take the little path running beside a stream. At the watersplash turn right up Brookley road and left into the car park.

Brockenhurst has many other fascinating corners to explore, particularly to the north opposite Brockenhurst College and around the Balmer Lawn Hotel. The Hotel served as Marshalling Area Headquarters for the D-Day landings in 1944. The troops erected an inn sign 'The Duck and Ducklings' showing a duck leading her family into the water.

Near the hotel in Balmer Lawn Road you will find New Forest Wagons. From here you can enjoy a leisurely wagon ride through the Inclosures from Easter through to November. Their telephone number is Lymington 23633. Close by there is an excellent campsite at Hollands Wood.

Walk 10

BROCKENHURST AND THE BOLDRE RIVER: IN THE STEPS OF 'BRUSHER' MILLS AND W H HUDSON

Starting point: Car, bus, train: Brockenhurst Station.

Distance: 6 miles.

Campsite: Hollands Wood, Brockenhurst.

This is a fascinating and unusual ramble. We see some of the most beautiful Forest countryside as we walk through great woods of beech and oak and follow the Boldre river. But we also see some of the more hidden delights of the Forest which contribute to its magic. We visit the oldest church in the Forest where there is a carving of a famous snake-catcher, 'Brusher' Mills, and explore one of the great

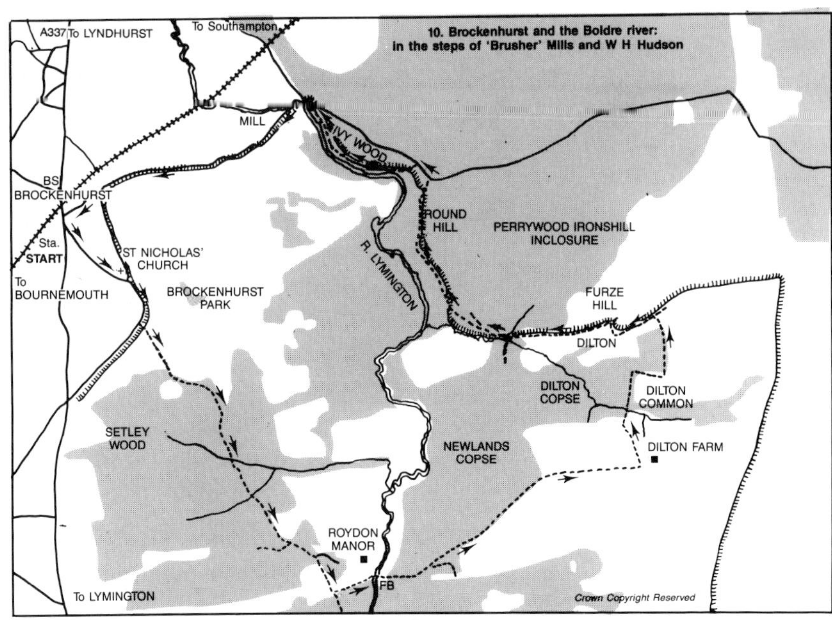

Additions to Key:
Sta. *Brockenhurst Station*
FB *Footbridge*

For general Key see p. viii

parks surrounding what was in former times a powerful manor. Few people knew the Forest as well as W H Hudson, the naturalist, or wrote about it with greater perception. We pass Roydon Manor which he described in his delightful book *Hampshire Days* and follow in his footsteps beside the Boldre river.

Our starting point is Brockenhurst Station. The distance round is about six miles, but allow a whole morning or afternoon for this walk as there is much to see.

From the Station, walk towards the crossing over the A337, past the Morant Arms. Cross the line and walk a few yards along the main road in the direction of Lymington. On the left you pass Mill Lane, the B3055 to Beaulieu (we come down Mill Lane to join the main road here at the end of our walk). A little further on you come to a second, smaller road on the left signposted to St Nicholas Parish Church. Follow this narrow lane as it curves uphill between high hedges spiked with blackthorn and twisting sprays of honeysuckle.

Brockenhurst Church, like all Forest churches, stands on top of the hill to serve as a landmark for travellers. It is the most ancient church in the New Forest. There was a Saxon church here (some Saxon herring-bone masonry will be found in the lower part of the wall between the south doorway and the east end of the Nave) and the *Domesday Book* records the existence of a church at 'Broceste' which is how the Norman scribes spelled the name of the village. The oldest part of the present building dates from the twelfth century. The south doorway with its lovely semicircular arch, chevron mouldings and scalloped capitals shows Norman work at its best. The font, a lead-lined bowl of Purbeck stone, is also Norman. Among many other interesting features is a charming curtained 'Squire's pew', like a small boxed-in room with seats all round. It is easy to imagine Addison's Sir Roger de Coverley, sleeping peacefully through the sermon in such delightful seclusion!

As you approach the south porch, on the left is an enormous yew. The creased and pleated trunk measures fifteen feet round. It deserves its mention in the *Domesday Book*.

I walked down the hill to the east side of the churchyard to see the beautifully kept memorial to the New Zealand and Indian soldiers who lie there. Brockenhurst played its part in both world wars; during the first it was the home of a base hospital.

I then had another look at the headstone of a local Forest personality, 'Brusher' Mills. His grave is in the north-east corner of the churchyard and you will recognise it by the carving of 'Brusher' on the headstone. 'Brusher' was what the Romanies call a sap engro — a snake catcher. He was called 'Brusher' because another of his occupations was to sweep the loose snow off the ice on Brockenhurst pond for skaters. But he made his living from the adders he caught in the Forest. C J Cornish, writing about the Forest in 1894 describes 'Brusher' as 'a strikingly handsome man slung all over with bags of sacking . . . from his chest hangs a pair of long steel forceps. He carried a light stick with a ferrule, into which when he rouses a snake he puts a short forked piece of hazel wood and darting it forward with unerring aim, pins the adder to the ground. Stooping down he picks it up lightly with the forceps and transfers it to his sack'. The ointment made from adder fat was good for 'sprains, black eyes, poisoning with brass, bites by rats and horses, rheumatic joints and sore feet in men and dogs'. He loved animals and cared for any sick ones he found. As a sideline he would sit by the road and entertain travellers on their way to Bournemouth with the snakes he kept in his pocket. His headstone shows him holding a handful of lively-looking snakes outside his Forest home, which, like the charcoal burners' huts, was a simple wigwam of branches covered with turf. One evening he returned home to find his hut destroyed by vandals. It is said that this so upset him that he became ill and died shortly afterwards, but he will never be forgotten; he has become part of Forest folklore.

From the Church, follow the road as it bears right. Past the corner you will see a bridleway leading from the road on the left, opposite a farm entrance. It runs between hedges with two sets of wide gates either side. Turn left and follow this path, bordered with ancient oaks running along the southern edge of Brockenhurst Park. This is part of the land belonging to Brockenhurst Manor which once stood here whose history, like that of the church, can be traced to the *Domesday Book*.

In Norman times the Lord of this Manor enjoyed many privileges. He could retain his land and exercise his rights of common to graze his animals and gather fuel, in the words of Domesday, 'quit and free from Verderers and foresters without hindrance from the King'. But conditions were attached. During the reign of Henry II the Lord of the Manor, William Spilman, was required to entertain the King when he came hunting. His son, also William, was required to serve the King for eleven days in the event of war. A branch of the most recent holders of the Manor, the Morant family, still lives in the area but the old Manor itself has been pulled down. A charming publication by the WI, *It Happened in Hampshire*, tells us that in 1812 a Dame's School was established in Brockenhurst by Lady Caroline

Morant. Miss Ash, a lame girl of eighteen from London, was installed as Head-mistress in one of the largest cottages where, for fifty years, she ruled with a rod of iron. On Sundays she accompanied her scholars to church in her donkey cart, the girls in uniform made by themselves from material provided by Lady Caroline, with muslin scarves and straw bonnets tied with pink and white checked ribbon. Every year they visited the Park for the school treat. At the head of the children's procession rode Miss Ash, the donkey dressed fore and aft in thick white cotton trousers tied with blue and yellow ribbons, the Morant colours! A former scholar of this severe lady reports that the girls had their aprons pinned to Miss Ash's and were made to kneel upright. The game was to fall over thus ripping off the teacher's apron! They evidently had a lively sense of mischief like one naughty boy who, locked as a punishment in a dark outhouse, discovered a store of apples in a corner. He took just one bite out of every apple!

Our path crosses a wide, grassy avenue. This is known as 'The Gallops' and was the training ground of 'Lovely Cottage' the Grand National winner. Follow the path as it runs to the left of a wood until the path leaves the farmland to wind downhill through Setley Wood. As I walked under the young oaks and beeches the air was noisy with the calls of rooks and pigeons. The path comes down to a stream, over a bridge, then up through a gap in the old Inclosure boundary to cross an open glade dotted with silver birches and willows. Cross another stream and climb uphill where you will see farmland again through the trees on your left. A wider track joins ours. Bear left for a short distance along this track until on the left you see the lodge by a private road to Roydon Manor. Follow the foot-path sign straight on until you come to another gate on the left. Although unmarked when I last came this way, it is a public bridlepath. Turn left, through the gate, and follow this path past Roydon Manor to cross the Boldre river into Newlands Copse.

As we pass this lovely seventeenth century house I must introduce another fascinating person who loved the Forest, W H Hudson. He came to live at Roydon Manor at the turn of this century. Perhaps better known as the author of *Green Mansions*, he was passionately interested in wildlife, making his own observations of his surroundings which he recorded in his book *Hampshire Days*. Originally this was a Manor House, but when W H Hudson lived here in 1902 it had been turned into a farm. He notes the date of the house, 1692, cut in a stone tablet in one of the rooms. Today the house has been restored from the rather ramshackle state he describes in *Hampshire Days* but still looks very much as he pictures it: 'never have I known any human habitation, in a land where people are discovered dwelling in so many secret, green, out of the world places, which has so much of nature in and about it . . . a small old picturesque red-brick house with high pitched roof and tall chimneys, a great part of it overrun with ivy and creepers, the walls and roof stained by time and many-coloured lichen to a richly variegated greyish red'. By his front door, he writes, 'a tiny gold crested wren sat on her eggs in her little cradle nest suspended to a spray of yew'. Small insects fascinated him. Observing that female grasshoppers were often ignored by the males and often sat patiently alone for hours, he carried one into the house on a wild rose branch. There she remained for sixteen days. When she had eaten all the berries on her branch, he kept her alive with a varied diet which included bread and butter pudding and ginger beer!

Below the Manor you cross the Boldre — or Lymington — river by a wooden footbridge. Looking at the water, it is exactly as W H Hudson describes it, the colour of old sherry. Climb through the wood and walk along the edge of Newlands Copse. At the top of a rise, when the path divides, keep straight on (left fork). Go through the gate at the end of the wood and take the track straight ahead which runs over farmland towards Dilton farm. Just before the farm turn left following the bridleway sign. This brings you downhill to cross a stream. Follow the path as it climbs to run along the edge of Dilton Copse then turn right beside another little wood. Our way then turns left again to cross an area of marshy ground and climbs with the wood on the left and a little heath on the right. You pass some huts remaining from a military encampment here during the last war. When you come to a bridleway sign turn left and follow the concrete path. Soon you come to a gravel track leading ahead as the concrete bears right. It is marked 'No through road, Dilton only'. (The sign is partly obscured by gorse bushes.) Leave the concrete and follow this gravel track to leave the bleakness of the heath behind and walk along a green valley with the scattered cottages that comprise Dilton on your left.

Cross the stream and keep straight on into the wood, keeping the stream on your left. (Ignore the more obvious broad track bearing left into a wood which is a private nature reserve.) Keeping the stream on your left, follow the track through Perrywood Ironshill Inclosure, a beautiful oak and beech wood. You come to a glade by a magnificent oak tree. The river is close by. Turn right past the tree then take the left hand of the two paths you see ahead which runs close to the Inclosure boundary along its western edge.

As I walked this way, squirrels were busily hunting up last year's nuts and birds rose in fluttering whirls, calling shrilly at my intrusion. Two magpies flapped noisily away from me. Once these smart birds were rare in the Forest, but they are now back in large numbers. They were a favourite of the gypsies who used to keep them as pets.

Our track now becomes deeply rutted and runs close to the boundary fence. Beyond the fence, on the left, the ground falls away to give glimpses of the Boldre river. The woods thin, and you leave the Inclosure to cross a green lawn.

Go past the barrier ahead to the B3055, the road from Brockenhurst to Beaulieu. Turn left and follow the road for just a few yards until you come to a path leading left into the woods. Follow this as it takes you down to the Boldre river. With the river on your left walk along the bank through Ivy Wood. This is an enchanting woodland walk. Keep to the river bank (the path is narrow at times) until you come to a road junction with a bridge with white railings on your left. Turn left over the bridge and follow the minor road. The old mill is on the right and you can see traces of the former workings. You pass impressive park gates, a reminder that you are now skirting the northern edge of Brockenhurst Park. Opposite the gates is a cottage with a large 'M' for Morant above the door. The railway is over the fields to the right and after about half a mile you will see Brockenhurst Station ahead. Leave the B3055, Mill Lane and cross the main road back to the station.

• BURLEY •

Burley, in the south west of the Forest, is very much a walker's village. It has grown, as Forest villages do, in a relaxed way around its old manor and park forming several small communities. So just when you think you have found and finished with the village you go round a curve in the road, through a wood, or over the crest of a heath and there is another little green surrounded by cottages and more gates into thickly-hedged gardens. Burley is confined to the west by a high ridge of moorland giving magnificent views over the Avon valley.

Burley was once so remote that it was said to depend for its livelihood on its yearly crop of acorns and beech mast! Not so today. Its narrow main street facing the Cross is thronged with visitors. Souvenir shops display local crafts, paintings on velvet and oil paintings. Some of the houses are very old, half-timbered, with their original open fireplaces. At the top of the street, facing the Cross, behind a modern shop front is the building which a hundred years ago was the sole village shop, selling everything from bread and bacon to oil for the lamps and blacking for the kitchen grates. Close to the Cross stands the Queen's Head Inn, a meeting place for smugglers in days gone by.

Walk 11

DRAGONS, SMUGGLERS AND BATTLES LONG AGO: BURLEY MOOR

Starting point: Burley central car park (near the Queen's Head Inn). Bus: the Queen's Head, Burley.

Distance: About five and a half miles.

The name 'Burley' means 'a fortified place in a clearing' and in the past it was the scene of many conflicts. West of the village runs a high ridge crowned with the embankments of an Iron Age hill fort. Below the fort, a Saxon here-path, or war path, runs west to Ringwood in the Avon valley. The village was a favourite haunt of smugglers whose road we follow over the moor. And close by, on Beacon Hill, surely the most amazing fight of all took place when brave Sir Moris tackled the local dragon!

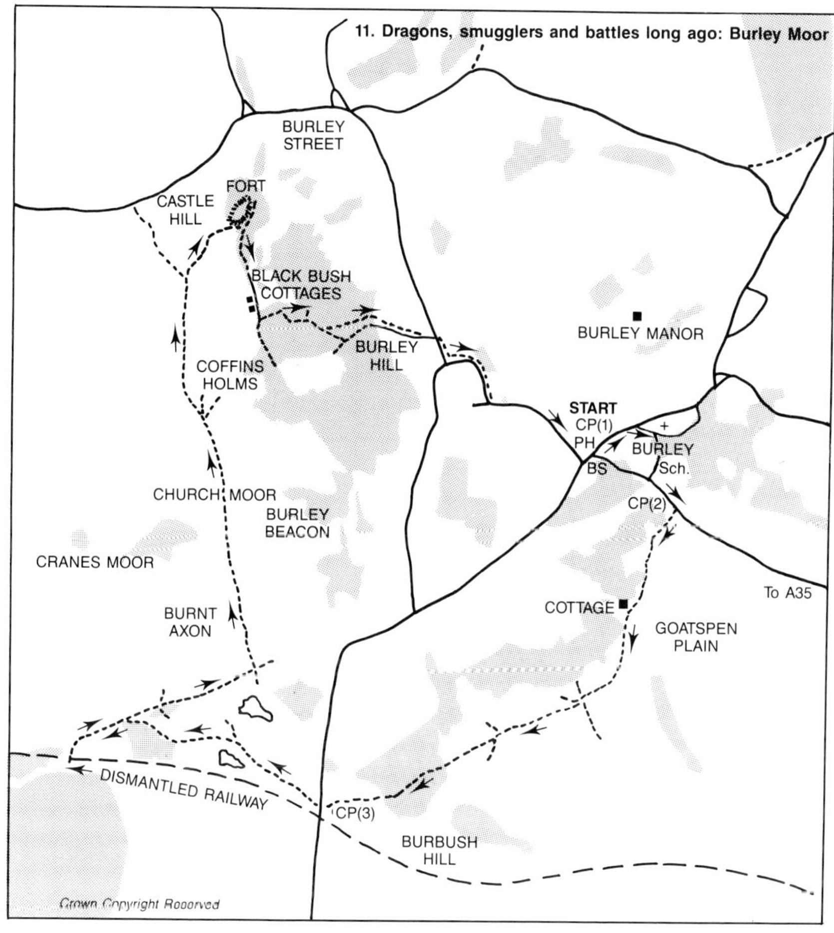

Additions to Key:

PH	*Queen's Head Inn*	CP(3)	*Burbush car park*
CP(1)	*Burley central car park*	Sch	*School*
CP(2)	*Burley car park (Turf Hill)*	*For general key see p. viii*	

I have planned this route to explore the scene of all these events. It is about five and a half miles round but as it involves a little gentle climbing and some wonderful viewpoints, allow a good half day, a whole day if you can. Burley, like Lyndhurst, is well known for its cream teas and it would be a pity to rush away from so good an Inn as the Queen's Head, close to which we begin and end our walk.

The Queen's Head stands at the junction of four roads at the head of Burley's main street. The bus from Southampton stops here. If you come by car you can park in the public car park close to the Queen's Head (not the Inn's own car park immediately beside it). A pleasant route to Burley is to follow the A35 (Bournemouth) road from Lyndhurst and in about four miles turn right for Burley at the sign. A lovely Forest road brings you into Burley village and the car park is on your right before you come to the Queen's Head. If that is full, drive up the road opposite the Inn where there are large car parks either side of the road.

If you stand with the front of the Queen's Head on your left you will see a minor road ahead called Chapel Lane (the road you followed if you came by my suggested route). Follow this road for a few yards until you see a track, Church Lane, leading right, up the hillside, signposted 'To the Church'.

Turn right and climb the short distance to the little Victorian church shaded by enormous yews and dedicated to St John the Baptist. It is probable there was a place of worship in Burley before 1550 as a deed of 1663 mentions a 'tenement called the chapel' and a field called Chapel Haye. This may have been a chapel belonging to the Manor, which after the Reformation was left derelict to be used as a cottage. Burley was originally part of the parish of Ringwood and was only separated in 1838 when Sir John Lefevre, Lord of the Manor of Burley, gave part of his estate called Barn Close for the first Anglican church. A small Dames school was set up in the churchyard.

From the church gate you have a fine view of Burley Manor in the valley, surrounded by parkland. Although the name Burley is not in the *Domesday Book*, the Manor was probably laid out in Saxon times and must have existed then as no further extensive grants of land would have been made once William the Conqueror had decided to enclose the Forest. The manor certainly existed in Norman times and was owned by the de Burley family for two hundred years until it was ceded to the King in 1388 when Sir Simon de Burley was executed in the Tower of London for alleged treason. Sir Simon was tutor to the Black Prince. For the following two hundred years Burley was a Royal Manor but in 1550 a Tudor house was built here owned by the Batten family. This was replaced by a Georgian house, burnt down in 1850. After the fire, Colonel Esdaile had the central part of the house rebuilt in Tudor style. The manor was requisitioned by the Army during the last war, the lake was drained and many fine trees cut down. One remains — a cedar, possibly about a hundred and fifty years old on the south lawn. Now the manor is a hotel.

Cross the road in front of the church and follow the path ahead, past the vicarage on your right, through the trees. You come out of the wood and keep straight on past the school. This leads to a minor road. Turn left and walk for about a hundred yards beside the road until you see a car park sign pointing right. Cross the road and follow the gravel track right past the nameboard for Burley car park.

Beyond a car free area barrier you will see our path, a white track leading south over the heath. Follow this straight ahead over all cross tracks. If you walk through the heather and gorse and small self-sown birches on a summer's day the scent from the fully opened flowers of the furze will rise through the warm air reminiscent of freshly grated coconuts. This heath above Goatspen Plain has a character all its own. The path dips and rises over shallow valleys and miniature hills presenting unexpected glimpses of a hidden Forest lawn, a half-concealed stream or a lonely wood.

Soon you come to a deeper valley with a white cottage beside an old barn standing to the right of our path. Turn left in front of the cottage and follow the track past a Forestry Commission barrier for a short distance along the valley. Then keep to the track as it bears right uphill and over the heath again. Across the heath on the right you will see the line of the old oak woods south of Burley.

Follow the main track over all crosstracks until you come to a point where four tracks meet. There are two tracks directly ahead of you. Take the left hand of the two paths and follow it downhill. A path branches right from our path, round the gorse, and, immediately after, our path forks. Ignore the first path and bear right at the fork in the direction of the minor road that runs from Burley due south to Thorney Hill. We aim to join this road at Burbush Hill car park just before the point where the road crosses a bridge over the disused railway. So keep to the track through a small belt of trees, over a green, to lead you past Burbush Hill car park on your left to the road. The railway bridge is on your left. Keeping the cutting through which the old railway runs on your left, cross the road and follow the path immediately ahead, running west, almost parallel with the railway.

You pass to the right of a small Forest pool where the path divides. Keep straight on (left hand of the two paths). This lovely path over the heath leads you downhill through a small glade, then up into a pine wood. Walk through the wood and downhill again where a path joins our way from the right. We shall be retracing our steps to this point later to follow this path, but the wood ahead is so lovely I would like you to see it first! Follow the path through some very tall Scots pines to another bridge over the railway. Pause here among these silent pine groves to absorb their scent and colour; their rich red bark contrasting with their dark glossy leaves.

Retrace your steps with Burley ridge directly ahead and bear left at the first fork. Shortly, you come to a point where three tracks meet. Keep going directly ahead following the centre path uphill. Follow this with Burley ridge still ahead of you. As you come close to the ridge you will see a pond over the heath on your right and meet a crossing track. Follow the path left, heading north across Cranes Moor. The long ridge formed by Burley Beacon, Burley Hill and Castle Hill now runs beside you over the heath to your right.

The whole area feels like an old battlefield and as John Wise the Forest historian tells us, place names seem to prove it. We find 'Greater' and 'Lesser Castle Fields' and 'Barrows' and 'Coffins'. On Cranes Moor you will see strange-shaped hummocks, a tumulus or ancient burial mound, and a curious wood of twisted oaks and thorns marked significantly on the map as 'Burnt Axon'. No doubt they were battle axes! Over to the right, Burley Beacon frowns down on us. Here signal fires were lit in times of danger and here, evidently, be dragons! There is a document in Berkeley Castle, of uncertain date, which tells the story of a fight between Sir Moris Barkley and a 'devouring dragon'.

The document reads: 'Sir Moris Barkley the son of Sir John Barkley, of Beverston, being a man of great strength and courage, in his time there was bred in Hampshire near Bisterne a devouring dragon, who doing much mischief upon men and cattel and could not be destroyed but spoiled many in attempting it, making his den near unto a Beacon. This Sir Moris Barkley armed himself and encountered with it and at length overcame and killed it but died himself soon after.' There are two Dragon Fields near Bisterne and the Green Dragon Inn at Brook probably is also a reminder of this legend for the redoubtable Sir Moris was also Lord of the Manor of Minstead and Brook. I saw no dragons but even today the area looks wild and remote enough to be the home of one!

Follow the track over Cranes Moor, past the foot of Burley Hill. This is one of several smugglers' tracks leading from Thorney Hill, over Cranes Moor then north to Picket Post (now beside the A31) where there is said to be a bricked-up cellar in which smuggled goods were stored. Keep straight on over all crosstracks. The path dips into a gully then climbs again. Follow the path for a short distance until at the foot of Castle Hill, on the open heath, the path makes a conspicuous fork. One way leads to the minor road you will see ahead, but our way bears right up the hill to the corner of an oak wood crowning our destination, the top of Castle Hill. So bear right at the fork. The slope is rather steep, but you will find, as with most Forest hills, you are soon at the top. As you climb higher you will cross ditches and embankments and if you look back you will see the two loaf-shaped hillocks guarding the approaches to this ancient hill fort.

A 'Castle' in the Forest means an Iron Age or pre-Roman fort or protected settlement. Today the encircling ditches and embankments remain, often enclosing a large area where the first settlement could be made and where later the whole village could gather with their animals for safety. Originally the embankments would have been crowned by high timber pallisades with strong gates. Dating back to about 500 BC, they indicate that the population of the Forest was fairly sparse. No Forest fort is comparable in size with those in Dorset.

Historians can tell us little about the part played by the Forest forts during the early days of the Roman invasion. Sufficient remains however to indicate that strategically the Forest was important as it lay directly in the path of the Roman advance towards Dorset. Later the area seems to have settled down peacefully under Roman rule. Pottery, made locally and at Sloden near Dockens Water, was exported to different parts of the Empire.

I sat on the ridges formed by the roots of some dwarf oak trees on the summit to enjoy one of the most wonderful views in the whole Forest area. Below you, rolling heaths spread in soft waves over the Avon valley to mist-blue hills merging into the sky. A little to the right a break in the outline of the heath gives a glimpse of the Wiltshire Downs and to the left you will see the tower of Christchurch Priory. Close by our hill runs a minor road from Burley through Crow to Ringwood; this is the Saxon warpath I mentioned earlier.

This road has been identified as a Saxon here-path by John Wise and Heywood Sumner, both noted Forest historians. 'Here' was the Saxon word for an army. According to the *Anglo-Saxon Chronicle* the New Forest was the scene of a major invasion by Saxon tribes under their leaders Cerdic and Cynric in AD 495. They landed at 'Cerdices ora', possibly Totton or Calshot, and advanced through the Forest to defeat the British at 'Natanleay', today called Netley Marsh. The name commemorates the British leader, Natan-leod. The area took some time to subdue for it was not until AD 519 that the Saxons inflicted a conclusive defeat on the Britons close to the Avon at 'Cerdices ford', today's Charford, not far from Burley.

Our return route is shorter as a good path runs from Castle Hill south along the top of the ridge past Black Bush, to Burley village. When you reach the top of Castle Hill, turn right and follow this path along the ridge. Just past Black Bush cottage look for a footpath sign and a stile on your left. Cross the stile and follow the woodland path to meet a minor road. Turn left to leave the wood, following the footpath sign downhill. Go over a crossing track and keep straight on downhill between the railings. The right of way has been re-routed to bring you out of the wood and to the left of what is now a private road to Burley Hill House. Follow the path beside the private road towards the iron gates leading to the road from Burley to Picket Post. Do not hesitate to go through the left-hand iron gate — you are on a public footpath. Walk down to the road past a rather inconspicuous footpath sign pointing back up our path on your left.

Turn right and walk a few yards along the pavement, then follow the footpath sign leading you to a safe and very pleasant path to Burley village. The path brings you down to the foot of the main street and on the right you pass an interesting milestone dated 1802. This seems to have been a busy year for milestone makers in the Forest as there is another one erected in the same year in Burley on the left of the road opposite the Queen's Head. It has the words 'Rest and be Thankful' carved on one side and 'Peace returned 27 March 1802' on another. This touchingly records the pause in the Napoleonic wars which followed the Treaty of Amiens.

Walk back up the main street towards the Queen's Head. At the top of the street you will see the Cross. Close by are several fascinating shops including the Burley Wagonette Shop where you can find details of a variety of wagon rides in this particularly lovely part of the Forest and buy souvenirs. To book in advance write to Burley Wagonette Rides, The Library, The Cross, Burley. To the left of the Cross is the Queen's Head and the bus stop and car park.

Walk 12

BURLEY VILLAGE AND HILL FORT

Starting point: Burley central car park (near the Queen's Head Inn).
Bus: The Queen's Head, Burley.

Distance: Six miles all the way round. There is an optional shorter walk of 3 miles.

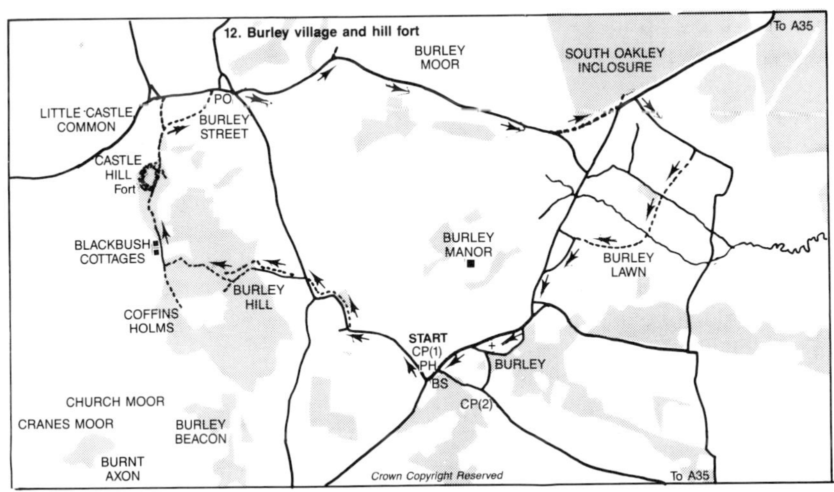

Additions to Key:

PH	Queen's Head Inn	PO	Post Office
CP(1)	Burley central car park		For general Key see p. viii
CP(2)	Burley car park (Turf Hill)		

There are several attractive routes to the Iron Age hill fort on the ridge west of Burley. This walk approaches the fort from the east and then takes you rambling round some of the byways of this intriguing village.

Park in the central car park, near the Queen's Head Inn or alight from the bus here. Turn right from the car park, past the Queen's Head, then right again to walk down the main street of Burley village. Keep on until by Clough Lane you see a footpath sign indicating a raised footpath to the right of the road. Follow this attractive path, shaded by chestnut trees, until it leads you down to the road again. Continue along the pavement for just a few yards and on your left you will see the gates of Burley Hill House. A public right of way leads through the right-hand gate (you will see an inconspicuous footpath sign pointing towards it) so do not hesitate to turn left, go through the gate and follow the footpath ahead by the drive. The footpath leads you uphill through a private wood. It is a tangle of old trees, carpeted with bluebells in late May and I have seen roe deer here. The path leads you between railings to a crosstrack. Go straight over and keep along the path to a stile by a footpath sign before a gravel track. Cross the stile to the track. It is worth pausing here for a moment to enjoy the view as you are now at the top of the ridge sheltering Burley and looking west over Vales Moor and the Avon valley to the soft blue line of the downs.

Turn right past Black Bush cottages. If you look over the gate just before the first cottage you will see an old well — the sort one would draw water from rather than throw pennies in and wish! You are now very close to the Iron Age hill fort which is on your left commanding a superb view of the Avon valley. As the trees thin on your left, turn left and follow one of the defensive embankments of the fort to enjoy the view.

The Forest hill forts are small compared with those in Dorset but in times of danger, this would probably have sheltered a whole village and their animals. Raised by the people of the Iron Age and dating back to around 500 BC, the fort was possibly the original Burley as the name means 'a fortified place in a clearing'. Below the fort you will see two small loaf-shaped hills which would guard the approach from the valley. The whole area must have been the scene of conflicts commemorated in the place names 'Burnt Axon' and 'Coffin Holms'.

Follow the embankment round to meet the gravel track again and turn left to continue our walk (the hill fort on your left). Follow the gravel track until you meet a joining gravel track on your right. Turn right and follow this track past a riding stables to meet the road in Burley Street. Turn right towards the little post office and village shop. All provisions can be bought here including the delicious local ice cream. If you wish, you can catch the bus back to Burley from the stop opposite the post office. You will be back at the Queen's Head in just a few minutes.

To continue our longer walk, turn left opposite the post office down Forest Road which is signposted 'Lyndhurst via ford'. Follow this minor road as it bears right to cross Burley Moor. The road soon becomes a real Forest way with moorland on the left and a single row of houses overlooking the moor on the right. Walk over the heath, following the line of the road for about a mile. The road then bears right. Before the bend, turn left just beside the first house you come to on your left. Walk over the green then follow the path along the southern edge of South Oakley Inclosure to meet a minor road. Turn left and follow the road for only a few yards before you turn right down a lane following the sign to Mill Lawn.

After about a quarter of a mile look carefully for a gate on your right with a footpath sign. The sign is half-buried in the hedge. Turn right and follow this good path which at first leads you between gardens. This brings you to a paddock. Keep straight on to a fence ahead which appears at first to block the way. However, as you approach the fence you will see a narrow way through. Now keep straight ahead through old-fashioned meadows full of flowers. Burley village has temporarily vanished!

A footbridge leads you over a pretty stream set with yellow flags and enormous kingcups. More footbridges guide your way over marshy areas to a stile. Climb the stile and cross a wider stream to follow the tree-shaded path ahead to a gravel track. Follow the track as it bears a little right towards a minor road. Just before you come to the road, turn left in front of some cottages and walk over the heath with the cottages on your right. Then bear right to meet the minor road. You can bear left along the road and follow it as it quickly brings you back to the car park close to the Queen's Head. Or, if you wish, keep to the road for only a short distance until it turns right. Follow the corner round until you see a track leading left. Take this uphill. When the path divides, bear right then left to meet a wide gravel track. Turn right along this to a lane. Follow the lane past the little Victorian church of St John the Baptist. Keep on down the lane to meet the road again. As you return to the car park you will have a fine view of Burley Manor on your right. The manor, dating back to Norman times, is now a hotel.

Walk 13

BURLEY BEACON

Starting point: Burley central car park (near the Queen's Head). Bus: the
Queen's Head, Burley.

Distance: 3 miles.

This is a pleasant short walk taking you to the southern part of the ridge sheltering Burley village, to Burley Beacon. There is a splendid view from the Beacon over the Avon valley.

From the car park close to the Queen's Head or bus stop, turn right. Do not turn right again down the main street but keep straight on past the post office with the War Memorial on your right along the Bransgore road. Follow this pleasant tree-shaded road until you come to Warne's Lane on your right. Turn right and follow the lane as it bears round to the left. When the lane turns left again continue straight on over the grass to a gate leading into a lane. Turn left and follow the lane until you see the Bransgore road ahead. Just before you come to the road turn right into Castle Hill Lane. Follow this attractive way and when the path divides keep straight on (left-hand path). Keep to the lane as it climbs to the top of the ridge and curves right to follow the crest through a wood. You are now on Burley Beacon and through the trees on your left you will have glimpses of the lovely view over the Avon valley I mentioned. On this hill, visible from the coast, beacon fires were lit in times of danger. And here, according to an old document, 'Sir Moris Barkley' of Berkeley Castle slew 'a devouring dragon'.

Just past a house on your left you come to a beautiful old oak wood and a Forestry Commission barrier. Turn left past the barrier to follow a woodland path

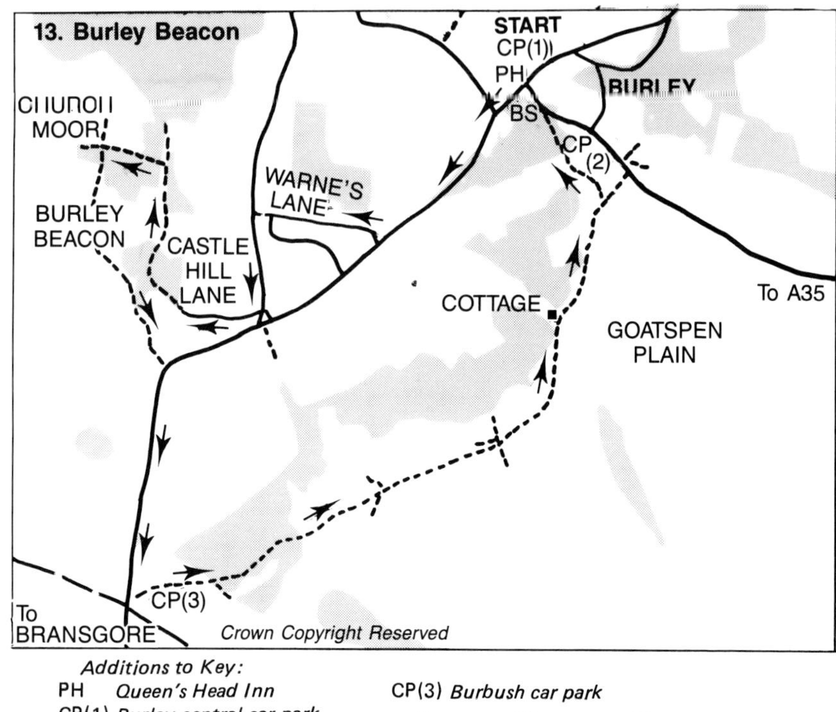

Additions to Key:
PH   *Queen's Head Inn*
CP(1) *Burley central car park*
CP(2) *Burley car park (Turf Hill)*
CP(3) *Burbush car park*
For general Key see p. viii

downhill through the trees. You are coming down towards Cranes Moor. As the trees thin you come to a crosspath. Turn left here. (You will see the garden of the house where we began our descent on your left.) Follow the path as it dips and climbs over the heath through a fringe of silver birches and oaks.

When you come to a minor road turn right and follow it. Soon you are able to walk over open heath beside the road. The line of the dismantled railway runs ahead of you. Just before you reach the embankment turn left and walk across Burbush car park. Keep straight on over the green beyond it and straight ahead through a narrow belt of trees. Now you will see two paths ahead. Ignore a very clear path winding a little right over the top of a small hill (Burbush Hill) and follow the path straight on keeping a line of woodland on your left. This is a beautiful moorland walk with views over shallow valleys to distant woods.

The track becomes clearer as you drop down into a little valley overlooked by a small Forest homestead at Shappen Bottom. Cross a stream here and keep straight on uphill, ignoring the wide gravel track running left. Leave a pole on your right and follow the path as it climbs steeply for a few yards, then levels to skirt the fringe of a holly wood. (Wood on your left.) Keep to the path as it leads you along the edge of the woods to the minor road and car park at Turf Hill. You can turn left at the road and walk the short distance back to our car park by the Queen's Head, or bear left through the car park at Turf Hill to pick up a path leading down to the village through the trees. This sunken track brings you down to the main street opposite the Queen's Head.

• THE HEART OF THE FOREST •

A short walk almost anywhere in the Forest can reveal an astonishing variety of scenery. Gravel plateaux, sandy plains, rich clay soils and marshes make their distinctive contribution to this diversity. In the central area, clay soils predominate and so it is here that we find most of the old woods of beech and oak — the 'ancient and ornamental' woodlands which are the pride of the Forest.

Here are the great 'pollards'. These trees have had their tops cut off before the year 1698 when the practice was declared illegal so now they sprout several thick trunks which spread huge elbows over the Forest floor. A pollarded oak can live for over eight hundred years! Oak woods with their open glades are the favourite haunt of the fallow deer with their Bambi-like fawns and the dainty red-brown roe. Insects abound in oak woods so birdlife flourishes. Among many fascinating species you will find the green and greater spotted woodpeckers and — in one of its last refuges — the lesser spotted or barred woodpecker. And hidden in the bracken you may come across the rarest of all Forest flowers, the wild gladiolus.

Walk 14

HOLIDAYS HILL AND THE KNIGHTWOOD OAK

Starting point: Millyford car park, near Lyndhurst. Bus: Burley Road Corner, off A35.

Distance: 5 miles.

Campsite: Holidays Hill.

This ramble of a little over five miles through the great woods around Lyndhurst takes you to one of the oldest and most well-known trees in the New Forest, the Knightwood oak. It is a wonderfully varied walk revealing the heart of the Forest right away from the crowded areas and busy roads. Our walk begins from Millyford car park, off that attractive minor road that runs from Emery Down to Ringwood. Leave Lyndhurst by the A35 in the direction of Bournemouth. Just outside the village, turn right at Swan Green for Emery Down. Drive through the village and immediately past the New Forest Inn turn left, following the road signposted Bolderwood and Linwood. About one and a half miles down this road you cross Millyford Bridge and the car park is on your right.

As this is a circular walk you can start from the bus stop off the A35 at Burley Road Corner and from Holidays Hill campsite. I will indicate these joining points

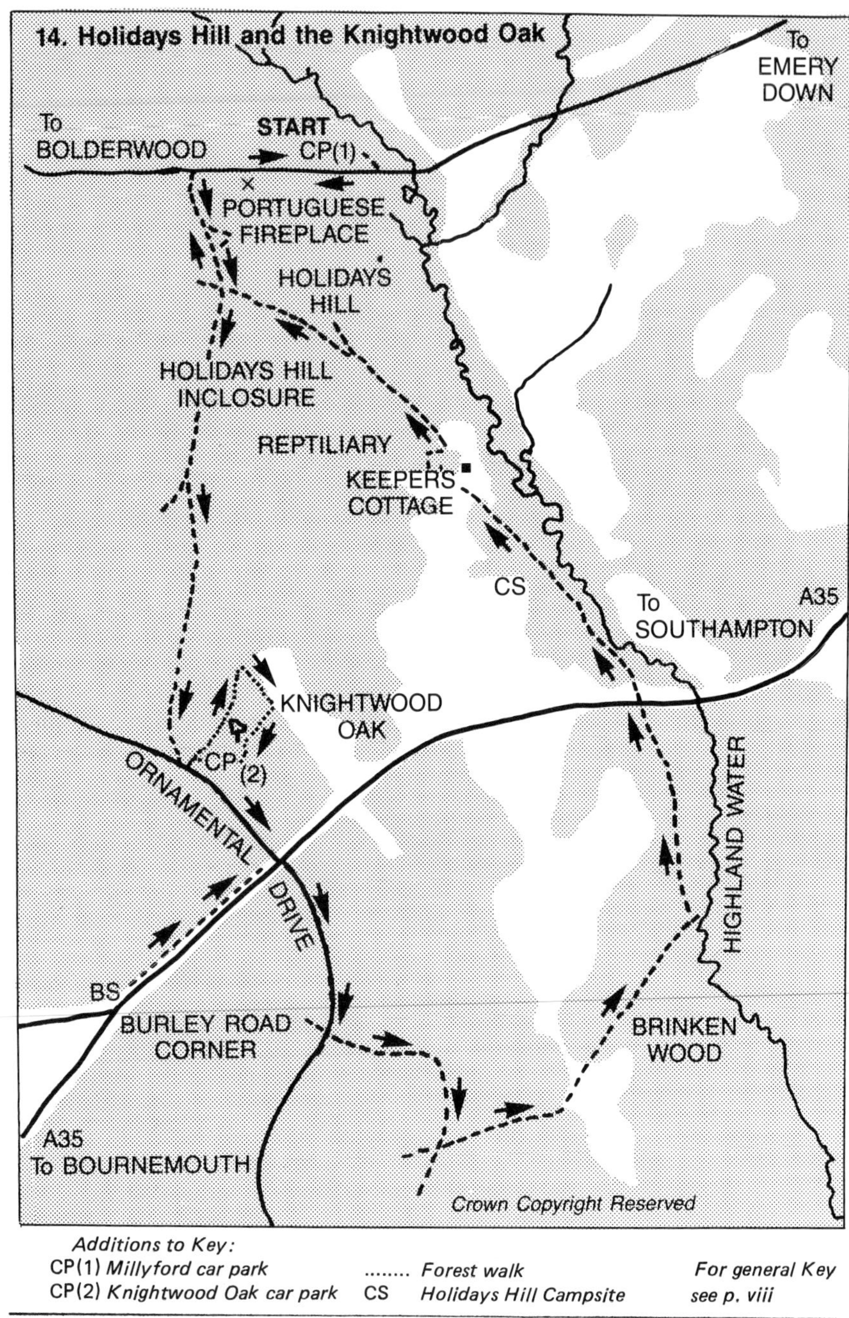

on the route.

Walk back to the road from the car park and turn right. Walk a short distance along the road, past a barbecue centre. You pass an interesting reminder of the first world war on your left. This is the Portuguese fireplace. Portuguese soldiers had a hutted camp here to help the local forestry workers during that war and the fireplace from their cookhouse was restored as a memorial to them.

A few yards past the centre, you will see a gate on the left and a gravelled track leading into Holidays Hill Inclosure. This is our way. 'Holidays Hill' used to be marked on the gate and also the date of the Inclosure — one of the first to be made in the Forest in 1676. This proves that, for all his faults, Charles II cared for the New Forest and was concerned about his stock of timber. In 1670 he appointed a Royal Commission to investigate the state of the Forest, which, partly as a result of the Civil Wars, had been neglected. Three hundred acres were enclosed as a nursery for young oaks. Now we can trace some survivors in glorious woods like Holidays Hill.

Walk along the gravel track through mixed woods of oaks, beeches and pines until you come to a grass triangle. Follow the track that bears right. Our direction is due south, so at the next crossroads carry straight on downhill. On either side of the path runs the line of the old Inclosure boundary, now a fraction of its former height, and over it bend the great boughs of ancient oaks.

When the track divides leave the gravel and follow the green way bearing a little left. Cross a bridge over a tiny stream, then follow the path uphill into another magnificent oak and beech wood.

Through the wood our way leads to a minor road which is the northern branch of the Ornamental Drive. Turn left, and a short distance down the drive you will find one of the glories of the New Forest, the Knightwood oak. Turn left across the car park and walk over the green lawns to have a closer look at this wonderful tree.

It is very old — some folk even say it was growing here in the days of William the Conqueror! But it can certainly claim more than three hundred and fifty years of life. It is a hundred feet tall and twenty-three feet all the way round. It might well have grown taller if it had not been pollarded. At some time in its remote past the top of the tree has been cut off so that strong new growth has sprouted from the top of the trunk. But if it had been left to grow naturally it might not have lived so long as pollarding was supposed to rejuvenate a tree. The practice also provides yet another link with William the Conqueror. 'Pollard' is derived from 'poil', the Norman-French word for a head.

This kingly tree is now the centre of the suitably-named 'Monarch's Grove'. To mark the ninth centenary of the New Forest in 1979, HM The Queen and the Duke of Edinburgh planted an oak a short distance away. Around the Knightwood oak itself eighteen oak trees were planted to represent all the recorded visits of reigning monarchs to the New Forest from William I to Edward VII in 1903.

Looking at this tree, it is easy to see why our even more distant ancestors regarded the oak as the king of trees and worshipped their gods beneath its branches. Today, with our renewed interest in conservation, the oak must still be regarded as the monarch of the Forest. No other tree fosters so great a variety of wildlife. For example, the purple emperor butterfly still finds a home in the New Forest. The larvae hatch in willows, but the adults live on the tops of certain high trees known as 'master oaks'. And as if this did not make them difficult enough for us to spot, they are most active at sunrise! The Knightwood area is also the home of the rarest of New Forest flowers, the wild gladiolus.

From the oak you can follow a pleasant short trail — about twenty minutes — round the area. Follow the posts marked with yellow bands. This is quite suitable for prams and pushchairs. On your way back to the car park you pass the Knightwood oak on your right before coming to the oak tree planted by HM The Queen on your left.

To continue our walk turn left from the Knightwood car park and walk a little further down the Ornamental Drive until you come to the A35 (Bournemouth) road. (You can start the walk from here if you arrive by bus. The bus stop is by Burley Road corner. Follow the A35 from the stop for about half a mile to the Ornamental Drive.)

Cross the road into the southern branch of the drive. Walk down this minor road, cross a stream overshadowed with rhododendrons and laurels, and take the first track on your left leading from a barrier. Follow this track round a sharp bend to the right. Now you come to a crossroads. Turn left and follow the ride to a gate immediately ahead. Go through the gate into Brinken Wood. This is a strange spot of hummocky green lawns, oaks twisted and bent into a host of angular shapes, and groves of elegant silver birches. Keep straight on, crossing the bridge over a stream. Now follow the green path you see bearing to the left through the birches. This track leads through the most beautiful part of Brinken Wood to Highland Water where we turn left to follow the stream. Walk through the young birches fringing Brinken Wood and follow the path as it bears north-east through lovely oak and beech woods.

When you come to Highland Water, turn left and walk along the streamside, either along the bank or the green track short distance away which runs parallel with it. Highland Water stream leads you back to the A35. You will see a road-bridge with a keeper's cottage behind it. Turn left when you come to the fence for about fifty yards and you will come to a gate leading to the main road. If you follow the green track parallel with the stream it will lead you straight to the gate. Cross the road and walk through the entrance to Holidays Hill camping area. (If you are camping or caravanning here, you could start the walk from this point.) Follow the track to the keeper's cottage, beautifully situated behind green Forest lawns. This is one of several lodges for woodmen built beside the Inclosures early in the nineteenth century. Each lodge had its garden and a paddock for a cow and a riding pony. Go through the gate. Walk past the cottage then turn immediately right through the gate following the directions for the reptillary which you pass on your right.

The best time to see the snakes is a really warm summer's day. All our three native species are represented: the harmless olive-green grass snake, the rare smooth snake, and our only poisonous reptile the adder, distinguished by zig-zag markings down its back. Adders, or vipers, are common in the New Forest but there is no need to fear them as they are quick to get out of our way. I read a story about a very greedy New Forest snake in *It Happened in Hampshire*. Apparently a girl with a bowl of porridge for breakfast allowed a snake to share it with her, dividing the portion equally. But the snake soon gobbled its porridge and began to eat hers. This made her so angry that she pushed it away exclaiming 'Eat your own side, speckleback!' This has become a local expression to apply to anyone who wants more than his share!

Go through the gate just past the reptillary into Holidays Hill Inclosure and follow the gravel track straight ahead for a short distance. Look for a small green track leading left through the pine trees and take this enchanting path — just one of the Forest's many magical ways. This leads you quickly to the gravel track we followed at the start of our walk. Turn right when you reach the gravel track. (If you are walking back to Holidays Hill campsite or to the bus stop on the A35 you will of course turn left along the gravel track to continue the route.) Walk past the green triangle of grass, and leave Holidays Hill Inclosure by the gate you originally entered. You are now back on the minor road from Emery Down to Ringwood. Turn right and walk the short distance back to Millyford car park.

Walk 15

MINSTEAD AND FURZEY GARDENS

Starting point: Bus and car: the Trusty Servant Inn, Minstead.

Distance: About two miles, but a great deal to see so allow a half day.

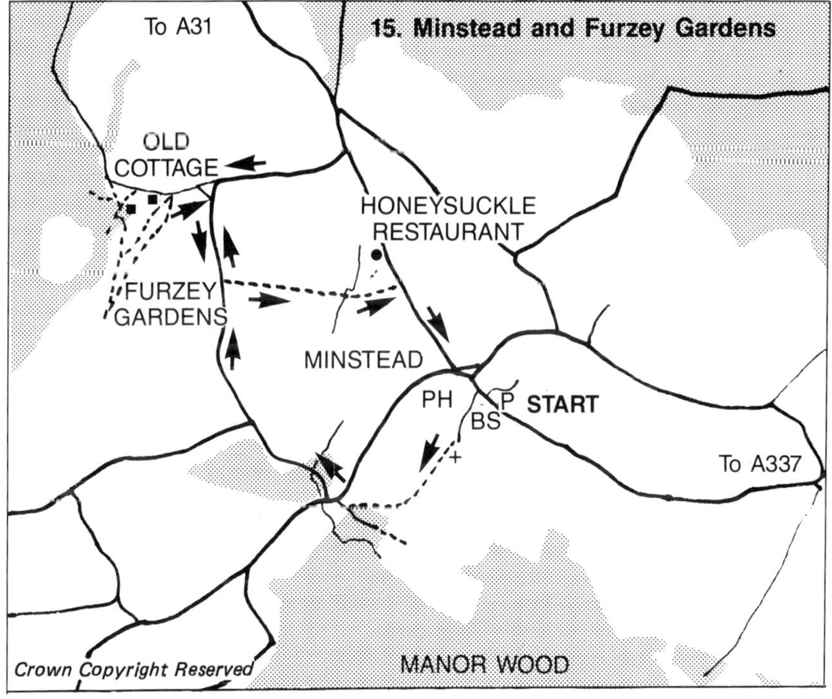

New Forest gardens, with their massed rhododendrons and azaleas, are at their most beautiful in spring. This walk takes us to one of the loveliest — Furzey Gardens. We start from Minstead, an old Forest village which is mentioned in the *Domesday Book* and called 'Mintestede', the place where mint grows. It lies just to the north of Lyndhurst around a network of minor roads between the A31 and A35. From Lyndhurst take the Romsey road (A337) and turn left for Minstead after about a mile and a half. Driving from Southampton follow the road to Cadnam then take the A31, turning left for Minstead two miles after the roundabout. Our destination is the Trusty Servant Inn. The inn stands beside the village green and opposite there is room to park. Buses stop close by.

Before we start our walk, have a look at the large and most unusual sign outside the inn. This depicts 'the trusty servant'. He is a pig, with a padlocked snout so that he cannot disclose his master's secrets, and hare's feet so that he can run errands quickly. It is copied from a picture in Winchester College and their motto 'manners makyth man' appears in the corner.

Leave The Trusty Servant on your right and follow the little road which leads uphill in front of it, signposted 'To the Church'. Overlooking the green on your left is the village War Memorial and close by an old well with a wooden cover. On your right you pass an interesting building. This was built in 1897 as Minstead Technical School on a site presented by H F Compton of Minstead Manor to commemorate the sixtieth year of Queen Victoria's reign. At the top of the hill stands Minstead church, one of the most fascinating in the whole New Forest area. It is built of traditional Forest materials — wattle filled in with rubble and daub. Stone could only be spared for the arches and corners of the main walls. Originally it was thatched and some of the old thin rafters that supported the thatch have been found above the present barrel roof. The archway over the north porch was carved early in the thirteenth century and is flanked by two heads, one most delicately carved and the other a much rougher version. Perhaps they are the work of a master and apprentice. Inside the church is a very rare three-decker pulpit. The sermon was preached from the top level, the Scriptures were read from the second. The lowest level was reserved for the parish clerk who had only an Amen to say occasionally. The family of Castle Malwood House, a mile or so away to the north-west of Minstead, had their own private pew. It is more like a cosy sitting room with a fireplace and its own entrance from an outside staircase. An inscription on the gallery states that in 1661 a certain Thomas Brown left money to be spent on bread for the poor of the parish. This charity is still administered on New Year's Day. Arthur Conan Doyle lived in the parish at Bignell Wood and his grave is in the churchyard. He features Minstead in his book *The White Company*.

Leave the churchyard by the lych-gate. A path runs from the road beside the church on your left. This is our way. With the churchyard — brilliant in Spring with crocuses and aconites — on your left, go through the gate and follow the path with the hedge on your right. The path leads you a little downhill towards Manor Wood. Go through the gate into the wood and follow the good path through the coppiced hazels, oaks and beeches. Go through the gate out of the wood and turn right to meet a minor road. Across the road, a little to your left, just before a crossing over a stream, you will see a sign pointing up a lane to the right signposted Furzey Gardens. Before turning right you might like to pause for a moment on the little footbridge to look at the narrow Forest stream as it cuts its way through green lawns shaded by oak trees.

Follow the lane uphill past a pretty thatched house on the left. Soon, a little to your left, you will see the long thatched roof of the large house in the centre of the gardens. Pass the first turning on the left and keep straight on. Soon you will see the lovely water gardens of Furzey on your left and come to a left turn by a grassy triangle signposted 'Furzey Gardens'. Follow the sign and after about fifty yards you come to the entrance to the gardens. (There is good parking here if you wish to come by car. Drive past The Trusty Servant in Minstead towards the A31 and take the first turning on the left which will lead you straight to Furzey.)

By the entrance gate is a good map of the gardens. They are open throughout the year and whenever you go there is always colour and interest. To ensure that some of these exotic plants would flourish, extra soil was brought here by horse and cart. One very rare azalea is said to have come from the garden of the Emperor of Japan. The Calico bush or *Kalmia latifolia* grows profusely here, its clusters of pink, star-shaped flowers have a particularly clean and fresh look, exactly like well-starched calico. In spring the grass is bright with drifts of butter-yellow cyclaminus daffodils and purple crocuses. The charm of Furzey is that there are no sharp divisions between garden and forest; it merges almost imperceptibly into the meadows and woods which surround it.

But Furzey has more to offer. A four-hundred-year-old cottage on the estate was recently saved from demolition and is now carefully maintained so that visitors can explore it and see how New Forest workers once lived. Downstairs there is a kitchen and a parlour. The parlour has been partly modernised and is used as an office, but the kitchen, with its enormous open fireplace, is unchanged. High up the chimney is a rail where the cottagers hung their bacon to smoke. In the hearth is an assortment of sixteenth- and seventeenth-century kitchen utensils. To one side is a large, circular bread oven and behind the oven part of the original wattle and daub of the cottage walls can be seen, built on a low brick foundation. New Forest cottagers built their homes out of whatever came easily to hand and the roof beams and upstairs flooring are made from old ship's timbers from the Tudor shipyards at Lymington. A narrow scullery and pantry, with an enormous flour bin in it, run the length of the outside wall. Upstairs, there are only two very small bedrooms and yet a family of fourteen children once lived here. The children slept on straw on the floor, with the younger ones in the middle. The last of the 'children' died in 1942.

By the cottage is a large gallery displaying a wide variety of local arts and crafts including pottery, woodwork, wrought iron and paintings, all capturing the special atmosphere and charm of the Forest.

We return to Minstead by a slightly shorter route. Retrace your steps, turning right as you leave the gardens, then right again by the first sign in front of the grassy triangle. Walk along the lane past the water garden on your right. About a hundred yards further down the lane look for a small half-hidden wooden stile and footpath sign on your left. Cross the stile and walk straight ahead keeping the hedge on your left down the field. Cross a little stream by a plank bridge and climb the small wooden fence to continue up the field ahead still keeping the hedge on your left. This quickly brings you to a stile and footpath sign and a minor road. Our way is right here but if you would like refreshments turn left a few yards up the road to the Honeysuckle Restaurant.

To continue our walk turn right from the stile and walk down the minor road. Almost immediately you will see the Trusty Servant Inn directly ahead. If you miss the stile, retrace your route by the church; it is only fractionally further. This circular ramble includes the church and the gardens and is about two and a half miles.

Inside the Trusty Servant, Mrs Mills told us about some of Minstead's present-day activities. At Christmas there is a large tree on the green and everyone gathers round it to sing carols. There is a bonfire and the old Mummers Plays and Morris dancing have been revived. Celebrations are held at Whitsun and Easter. Here again is that happy mixture of the old and the new so characteristic of the Forest.

Walk 16

THE ORNAMENTAL DRIVE AND OBER WATER FOREST TRAIL

Starting point: Puttles Bridge car park, off the Ornamental Drive.

Distance: Short walk about a mile, longer walk about two miles.

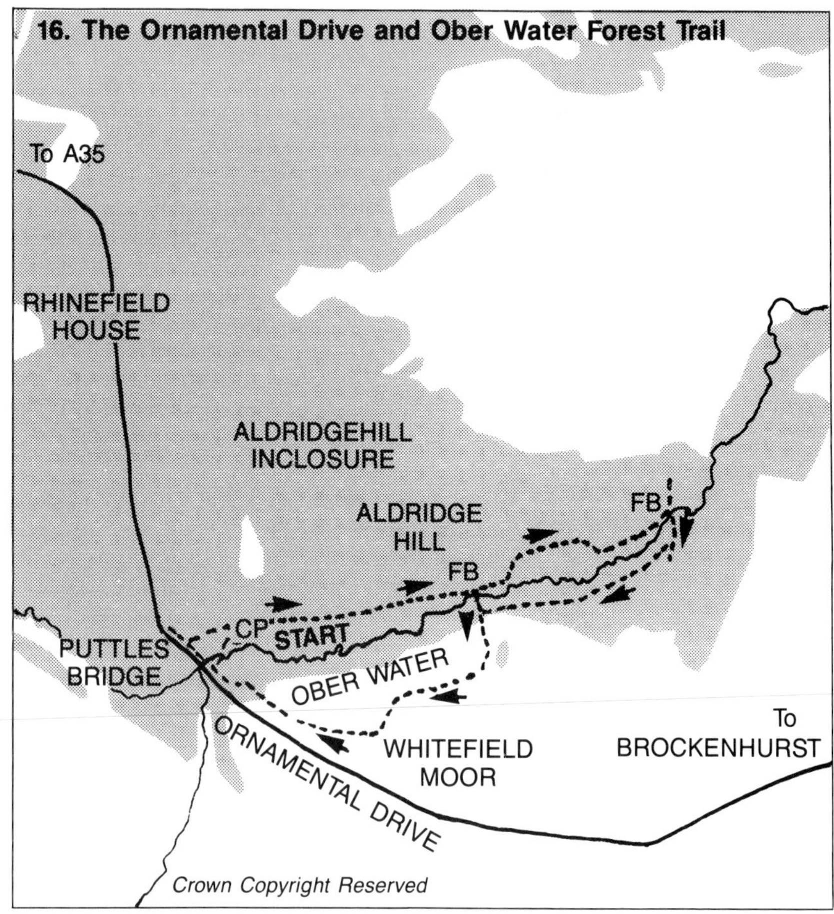

Additions to Key:
FB *Footbridge*
CP *Puttles Bridge car park*
For general Key see p. viii

Ober Water Forest Trail is a clearly marked walk along the banks of a small stream which winds round roots of trees and islands of shingle shaded by mixed woods of oak, beech and pine. Ober Water is typical of the streams in the central part of the Forest that run over clay — reddish-brown in colour and liable to flood and wash their banks bare of vegetation. Like the other Trails laid and maintained by the Forestry Commission, the path is well-drained, there are parking and picnic areas and information posts at interesting spots along the route. (Details of the other trails can be obtained from the Information Centre in Lyndhurst car park and from dispenser posts at the start of the trails.)

At Ober Water you can choose between a short walk, which takes about thirty minutes and is indicated by posts with yellow bands, and a longer one, which takes about an hour to complete if you walk at a leisurely pace. This is marked by red bands.

The Ober Water stream rises within the Forest itself at Backley Plain and flows south to join the Lymington river above Bolderford Bridge. There are two possible starting points for this trail, both leading off the southern part of the Ornamental Drive. From Lyndhurst follow the A35 in the direction of Bournemouth and after about three miles turn left into the Ornamental Drive.

This southern part of the Ornamental Drive originally formed the approach to Rhinefield House which we shall see later. The splendid avenue is formed by exotic trees most of which were planted in 1859. Among these you will see Redwoods, Black Spruce and Spanish Fir. Drive past the entrances to the trails north of Rhinefield and cross the Blackwater stream. The road curves sharply left and if you look to your right you will see Rhinefield House standing on a rise. The present house, now a hotel, was built in mock-Tudor style in the nineteenth century. However, it stands on a site with a history dating back to William the Conqueror who had a hunting lodge here. A larger fortified house was built on the site and used as a hunting lodge by Charles II. Later the old house became the home of the Master Keeper and in 1811 the Duke of Cambridge.

About half a mile further, almost at the edge of the woods, you come to Puttles Bridge car park on the left. Our walk starts here. As you drive in, the Ober Water stream, crossed by a wooden footbridge, is on the right. We return over the bridge but to begin our walk follow the ringed posts along the gravel track straight ahead with Aldridge Hill Inclosure on your left. When you come to a junction you have the choice of continuing straight on for the longer walk or turning right over a footbridge to follow the yellow signs only for the shorter walk.

For the longer walk continue by the stream for a short distance, then follow the trail as it turns left into Aldridge Hill Inclosure. Aldridge was planted as mixed woodlands after the fellings of World War I and is now a picturesque blend of oaks, beeches and pines of many varieties. Near a stand of splendid Scots pines is the stump of a tree riddled with the tunnels of the longhorn beetle. Look for woodpeckers here as these beetles are their favourite food. Apart from the large green woodpecker with his vivid colouring you may see a smaller relative, the great spotted or pied woodpecker. He is equally good-looking, black and white above with a bright crimson patch on his head and under his tail.

As we walked through the Inclosure on our last visit the rain, which had lasted all morning, stopped and a rather watery sun appeared. The bushes and small trees beside the path were hung with masses of raindrops which glistened like tiny crystals. We came to an area where the oaks and beeches allowed sufficient light to penetrate to encourage young beech seedlings to develop naturally from seed. However, many of the small trees were stunted and broken — a sure sign that these woods were the home of fallow deer who had enjoyed grazing on their succulent new growth. We did not see any deer but that may have been because these beautiful but destructive animals dislike moving about in showery weather even after the rain has stopped. They object to the cold drops falling on them off the branches of trees!

Our trail turns to the right to cross the stream by a wooden footbridge. This is the right place to pause, lean on the rail and look for fish. Plenty of minnows — known locally as minnies — dart about in the shallower water and although they are shy and difficult to spot, you may see some of the small brown trout that live in these Forest streams. Across the bridge, the track turns right to follow the other bank. It is possible to miss this turning as a wide track continues straight ahead, but look for the marker post just around the corner. Follow the stream again; this time the path hugs the water's edge. There had been so much rain before our visit that the stream beside us was very full, its reddish-brown water rushing along in quite a wild fashion, more like a northern river than a gentle Forest brook. It was carving ever deeper curves into the soft parts of its banks and washing the soil away from around the tree roots. Sometimes after very heavy downpours, these Forest streams flood dramatically carrying debris of all kinds before them. When the water subsides this debris is left hanging in the trees and bushes.

Our way now turns left to leave the wooded streamside and bring us out onto the open heath. Over the heath the trail bears right and you will notice Forest ponies happily grazing on a level expanse of grassland surrounded by the heather and gorse covered heath. During the last war, parts of the Forest were ploughed and grew corn for the first time. Now the Forestry Commission maintain these areas as open grassland for the benefit of the Commoners' animals, which include the ponies. This grassland also provides what is known in the Forest, rather unexpectedly, as a 'shade', an open place where animals can congregate in summer to escape the attacks of flies.

From the gorse bushes along the path we were assailed by the anxious scolding of the stonechats who nest low down in the bushes. The stonechat has the local name of 'fuzz topper' and he is a smart little bird with an interesting way of jerking and flirting his wings and tail as he settles on the gorse. Although he sounds so bad-tempered he is the most useful of birds — an asset to any garden — keeping down the numbers of harmful insects.

Our track leaves the heath to enter another car park at Whitefield Moor. Cross the car park and pick up the trail again at the other side as the markers indicate. Now we cross an area of typical Forest boggy marshland but fortunately our track is well raised above it so we can walk dry shod and enjoy the fascinating plant and animal life on either side. Most of the small bushes are sweet-smelling bog myrtle, or to give this plant its old country name, the gold withey. Berries from this bush were once used in brewing the local beer. In this acid and infertile earth very few plants apart from willows can grow successfully but it is the home of a very unusual flower which has its own clever, if rather gruesome, way of overcoming the lack of nitrogen in the soil. This is the sundew. It has round sticky leaves held well up on strong stalks. When insects alight on these leaves they close up and the plant is able to absorb the nitrogen from the insects' bodies.

Soon you re-enter the woods and walk under pines again. The ground is littered with the remains of pine cones. Squirrels like to sit holding a pine cone in their hands and nibble the seeds out from between the scales. As far as I know, there are few of our native squirrels left in the New Forest but the greys are flourishing to such an extent that they have become a real pest to the forester. The grey squirrels did not, as is sometimes supposed, kill off the red. The Canadian newcomers happened to be much tougher, stronger and more resistant to a certain killer disease than our own red squirrel. To see red squirrels in the south you must go to the Isle of Wight or Brownsea Island in Poole Harbour.

Cross Ober Water by another footbridge and you are back in Puttles Bridge car park where we began our walk.

Walk 17

ROBIN HOOD COUNTRY:
DENNY WOOD AND BISHOP'S DYKE

Starting point: Shatterford car park, Beaulieu Road Station. Train: Beaulieu Road Station (between Bournemouth and Southampton).

Distance: 5 miles.

With all the bustle of life today, have you ever envied Robin Hood his free and easy sort of life among forest glades? If he was to come back with his merry men he might be sad to see how little remains of his beloved Sherwood but there would be no need for him to despair. A ride south to the New Forest and he would find just the country he was used to: wide lawns and ancient oaks, tangled holly thickets sheltering the deer, quiet ways into remote valleys. He might find a shortage of rich sheriffs and Norman knights perhaps — but apart from these minor problems he would feel at home here.

This walk takes us to real Robin Hood country, the ancient oak and beech woods of Denny. It is a ramble of about five miles, starting from Beaulieu Road Station which is easily reached by bus, rail and car. This small station (famous for its pony sales) lies in glorious country between Ashurst and Brockenhurst on that most useful line for walkers running between Southampton and Bournemouth.

To reach Beaulieu Road Station by car follow the B3056, the Beaulieu road, from Lyndhurst. After about four miles just before the road crosses the railway, you will see our starting place, Shatterford car park on the right. If you come by rail, the car park is close to the station, to the west of the road.

Several paths radiate from the car park. Ignore the obvious track which runs past a Forestry Commission barrier — that is our return route. Walk back to the large car park sign at the entrance, turn left and walk between the pine trees west, towards the open heath. The car park is on your left. After the pines, our way becomes a good track and easy to follows.

This treeless expanse of open moor appears rather desolate on a grey day, but it is a marvellous place for seeing wildlife. I first came here some years ago as a stranger, in late spring. I saw a large, brilliant yellow bird with jet black markings on its wings and tail flying in graceful curves over the low bushes. Another visitor who was watching it through field glasses told me we were watching a golden oriole. This exotic bird migrates through southern England in the spring

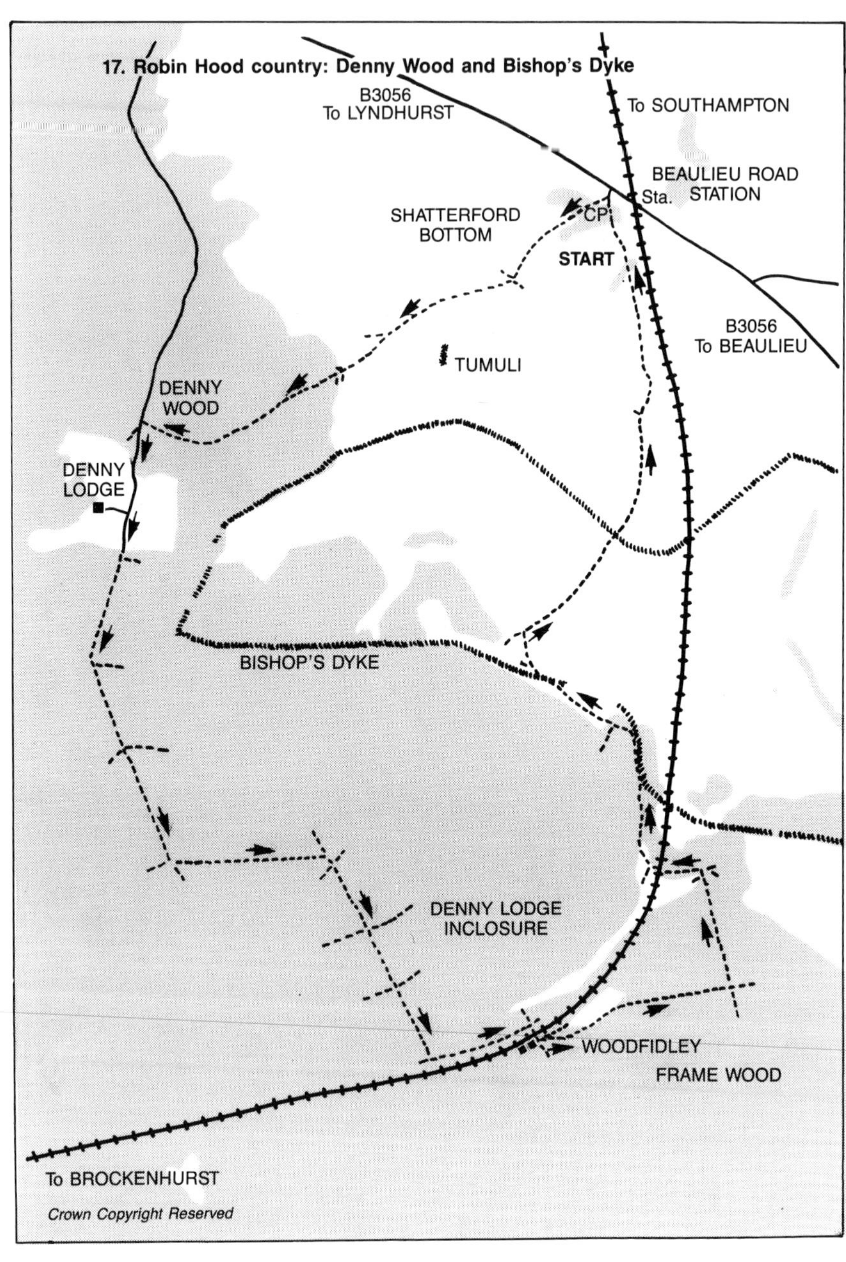

Additions to Key:
CP *Shatterford car park*
Sta *Beaulieu Road Station*

For general Key see p. viii

and occasionally stops for a few days' rest in the New Forest on his way to a warmer climate.

You pass three tumuli, or ancient burial mounds, on your left. When the path divides, follow the left-hand track. Ahead of you a misty fringe of trees forms the outline of Denny Wood. As you come closer to the wood the path divides again. Ignore the left-hand path and keep straight on over all joining tracks into this lovely wood. At first you walk through groves of self-sown silver birches and it is these delicate trees that have helped the oaks and beeches they shelter to achieve their full beauty. Foresters often make deliberate use of thinned birchwoods to protect young beeches and pines from strong winds and hard frosts. Denny Wood — perhaps the most beautiful of all the New Forest's 'ancient and ornamental' woodlands — is one of the last sanctuaries of that rare bird, the lesser spotted or barred woodpecker. He is smaller than the rest of the woodpecker family; only about five inches long, with distinctive bands of black and white across his back and wings which show up clearly against the tree trunks.

The track goes slightly uphill as you walk through Denny Wood, then becomes level before a small clearing. As you come into the clearing the track becomes in-distinct. Walk straight ahead, across the clearing to where the ground slopes a little downhill. Through the trees ahead you will see a minor road. Cross to the road. Turn left and follow the road downhill. (Ignore a track leading to a gate on your right.) Our track crosses a lush green valley with cottages tucked away among the trees. You pass Denny Lodge on your right which has a weather vane sur-mounted by a replica of a red deer stag. He stands, head into wind, as he would in the wild.

Go through the gate ahead into Denny Lodge Inclosure. Here, silver birches act as 'nurses' for pines. We are aiming for the railway as it curves due west for Brockenhurst. Follow the gravel track through the pines and turn left down the fourth ride that leads from it. The ride meets a T-junction. Turn right and walk over a crosstrack to the top of a rise. Go over another crosstrack and keep straight on down the green ride ahead. This leads you down to a gate before wide lawns crossed by the railway. Go through the gate and turn left to walk over the lawns, with the railway on your right.

The curves in the line here earned it the name of Castleman's corkscrew. Castleman arranged the line in this way to avoid cutting through the great woods around Lyndhurst, including Denny. As we look at the peaceful scene today it is difficult to imagine the horror which the coming of the railway aroused in many Forest people. Philip Klitz, in his book *Sketches of Life, Character and Scenery in the New Forest*, describes how the driver of the local 'neck-or-nothing', the fastest coach of its day, reacted to the coming of the steam trains. 'Will this rum-looking drag,' he inveighed, 'with its snorting breath and smoking chimbley convey its passengers in a body safely to the place named in the advertisements, or will it scatter their bruised and blackened carcases at some place on the line, or off the line, not mentioned in the bills?'

Follow the line to a crossing with a small cottage, Woodfidley. Cross the railway here and turn left. You will see two paths running roughly parallel with the railway. Take the right-hand path towards Frame Wood. If you look left, over the line, a few fine old beeches on the hill are all that remain of the once famous Woodfidley. But Forest folk still refer to 'Woodfidley rain' when they mean rain that is likely to last for some time. It is coming from the direction of Woodfidley, from the south-east.

Frame Wood is a quiet place, a blend of pines and oaks. Cross the wooden rails and walk on into the Inclosure. Turn left at the first crosstrack which leads to a gate facing the railway. Go through the gate and look for a bridge over the line on your left. Cross the bridge and take the right hand of the two paths you see ahead (not the track leading to a gate). Your path runs along the eastern boundary of Denny Lodge Inclosure with the railway over the heath on your right. This is a beautiful path; an embanked way beneath arches of fine trees including some splendid beeches, possibly more remnants of ancient Woodfidley. When the woods become more open with glades of silver birches keep straight on with the denser woodlands now on your left.

Soon you will notice a low, rounded earthwork steering a rather wandering course over the heath to cross your path in places. This forms part of the boundary of Bishop's Dyke, an area of marshy ground about a mile in length and half a mile wide, which, until quite recently, belonged to the Bishop of Winchester. John de Pontisarra, Bishop of Winchester, persuaded Edward I to let him enclose the land in 1284. The puzzle is, why should the bishop want this boggy waste, intersected with runnels and shallow pools? Was he a keen wildfowler who was after the best bit of snipe shooting in the area? The land may have been drier in the bishop's day and of course he could only have required pasture for ponies. Naturally, a Forest legend has grown up about this neglected inclosure. In ancient times, it is said, one of the prelates of Winchester was promised as much of the New Forest as he could crawl round on his hands and knees in twenty-four hours, the boundary to follow his route. Certainly the wavering course does suggest the route of someone proceeding with difficulty.

You meet a track leading left into the wood and right towards the heath. Turn right by a magnificent oak tree and follow the track over two bridges. The path climbs to lead you over the north-eastern embankment of Bishop's Dyke and now you will see Beaulieu Road Station over the heath ahead. Follow the good track as it turns north towards the station. You enter Shatterford car park along the path I mentioned earlier past the Forestry Commission barrier.

Walk 18

CASTLE MALWOOD AND THE RUFUS STONE

Starting point: Castle Malwood walk: Hungerford car park, off the A31, close to Castle Malwood. Rufus Stone walk: Rufus Stone car park, off A31. Bus (both walks): Castle Malwood, off A31.

Distance: Castle Malwood walk: 4 miles. Rufus Stone walk: 2½ miles.

The New Forest with its nine hundred years of history has more than its share of secrets. This walk, mainly through old woodlands, explores the most mysterious part of the Forest. Our starting point has the intriguing name of Castle Malwood. Close by, an event took place which still puzzles historians. Only the Forest knows the real answer! This was the death of William the Conqueror's favourite son, William Rufus on August 2, 1100. While out hunting in Canterton Glen an arrow,

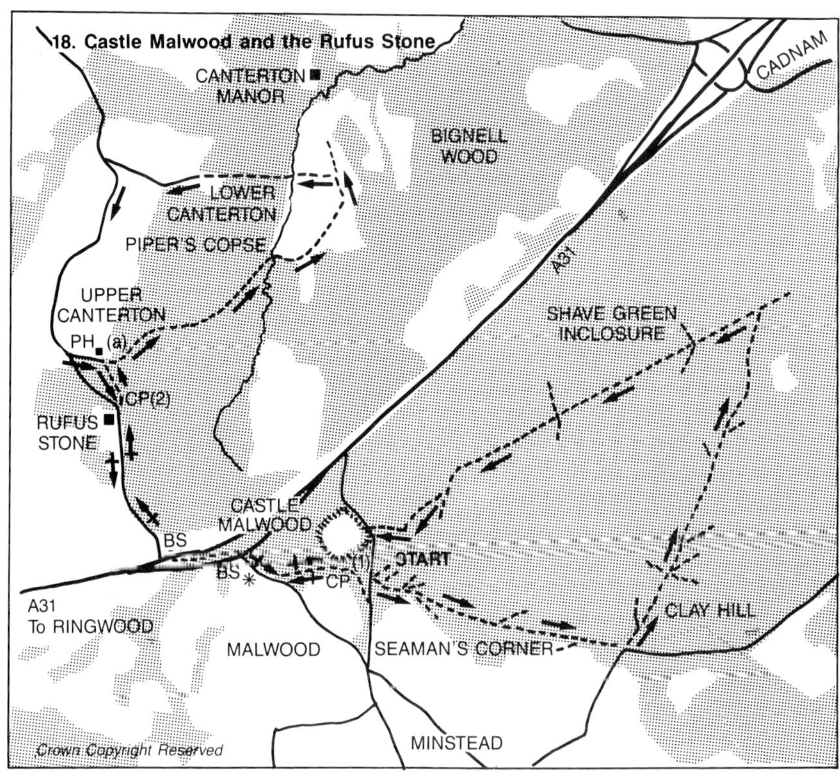

Crown Copyright Reserved

Additions to Key:
CP(1) *Hungerford car park*
CP(2) *Rufus Stone car park*
✳ *Road to Minstead and Lyndhurst*

PH *Walter Tyrrel Inn*
(a) *Cottage*
For general Key see p. viii

allegedly shot by a nobleman Walter Tyrrel, pierced his heart. An accident? Or was it murder? We visit the spot where he fell now marked by the Rufus Stone.

Tradition also tells us that the night before, William Rufus had slept at Castle Malwood. The King ate and drank regally — probably too well. The Saxon chroniclers (prone to exaggeration concerning the hated Normans) tell us that he awoke suddenly to see a vision of a stream of blood — his own — pouring from heaven and clouding the daylight. Next day monks came and gave him more warnings. He would not have improved his standing with his English subjects when he told them: 'Am I an Englishman, who puts faith in the dreams of every old woman?' He fortified himself with a few more drinks then went out hunting, never to return.

Historians may differ over the facts concerning his death and the spot where he fell may not be known exactly, but what is to exciting for us today is that the Forest remains much as he saw it. He would still feel quite at home among the woods and glades we walk through.

If you glance at the map you will see that our route divides into two walks so if you prefer you could walk through Shave Woods one day and through

Canterton Glen another. The distance round the combined walks is about six and a half miles; four miles through Shave Woods and about two and a half to visit the countryside round Canterton Glen. Allow a good half day for the whole walk.

Castle Malwood is beside the A31, Southampton–Ringwood road. If you are driving from Southampton, about a mile and a half past the Cadnam roundabout turn left down a minor road signposted Minstead and Lyndhurst. After about a quarter of a mile you pass the first houses in Minstead village and a signpost on your left. Do not follow the roads signposted but turn sharp left (the first lane on the left). About a quarter of a mile down this narrow lane you will see the gravel entrance to Hungerford car park on your left. There is no indication on the road of the car park but it is the first gravel entry. As you turn into the park you will see the car park name board. There is a lane to the car park directly from the A31, but as (at the time of writing) it is not signposted, it is safer to take the slightly longer route I suggest.

If you come on the bus from Southampton, you pass the minor road and stop close to the small lodge at the entrance to Castle Malwood. Walk back to the minor road signposted Minstead and Lyndhurst, and follow it right. Ignore the first lane on your left and look for a second smaller lane leading left, just before the Minstead sign. Turn left down this lane and when a track goes right for 'Hollybrae', carry straight on down the hill. When you come to a belt of trees keep straight on and Hungerford car park, our starting point beside Castle Malwood, is just beyond.

Encircling the hill to the left, if you stand facing the car park entrance and the minor road, you will see a deep ditch and embankment. This explains the 'Castle', a name given in the Forest to the remains of Iron Age hill forts. Within the embankment stands Malwood Lodge, built in 1884 in neo-Tudor style for Sir William Harcourt, then Gladstone's Home Secretary. It is on the site of a former simple Forest lodge and documentary evidence proves that in 1358 a lodge called Hardebourgh stood here. So there seems no reason to disbelieve the tradition that William Rufus feasted and slept here the night before his death.

To begin our walk return to the car park entrance and the minor road. Look over the road and you will see two possible paths leading ahead into Shave Woods. Follow the right hand of the two paths, directly opposite the 'Hungerford car park' sign. When the path divides, keep straight on. Through the trees on your right you will see the Inclosure boundary and glimpses of fields. Shortly you have a choice of three tracks leading ahead. Again, bear right towards the Inclosure boundary for a few yards. When the path divides follow the path bearing a little left, slightly away from the Inclosure boundary. You are now walking through the most lovely part of Shave Green Wood. Here and there among the soaring oaks and beeches are some ancient pollards. Pollarded trees are mostly over three hundred years old. Their main trunks have been shortened while quite young so that now they spread many twisting, curving trunks in all directions making shaded glades beneath them. Keep straight ahead with the Inclosure boundary and edge of the wood about fifty yards away on your right. When the trees begin to thin and the path divides keep straight ahead, following the right hand of the two paths.

When I came this way I stopped to look more closely at a much smaller tree, a lime, with silvery green leaves furry to touch. Lime trees like this one are fairly rare in the Forest and when you do see them they make a fresh cool contrast with the oaks and beeches. In Summer bunches of still tightly closed flowers hang like small tassels among the leaves. Limes are very useful trees. Most of Grinling

Gibbons' carving was in lime wood, and the bark can be made into ropes, nets, mats, even clothes! So when Lyndhurst was first settled — in the *Domesday Book* it is Linhest, wood of lime trees — the villagers would have made good use of their trees.

Soon you come to a more open area with green lawns dotted by fine oaks ahead. Cross the lawns to a gravel track. On the hillside to the right are a few houses and cottages and a large grey building, Minstead Lodge. Turn left along the gravel track and follow it past a sign 'Suters Cottage only' to meet a minor road. Just at the point where the gravel track meets the minor road you will see our path leading left from the corner. Turn left and follow this path, bearing slightly right at first up Clay Hill, ignoring all side tracks. When the path divides, keep going straight on (left-hand path) uphill. Arching boughs of tall unpollarded beeches meet over your head so that you feel you are walking in some vast green-roofed cathedral. Just before the top of the hill our path becomes level then follows the side of the hill for a few yards before descending to a small grassy clearing. Go over the clearing to meet a crosstrack. Beyond the crosstrack you will see two possible paths leading ahead. Follow the left hand of these two paths. The path is rather indistinct and when it divides keep going straight ahead along the left hand of the tracks. Pick your way round a large fallen tree and you now have a wide pleasant path flanked by beech trees.

Looking at these mighty beeches rising from their deep carpet of russet leaves, it is surprising to recall that this area of the Forest, between Romsey and Lyndhurst, very nearly became farmland during the reign of Queen Anne. Daniel Defoe, author of *Robinson Crusoe* and an indefatigable traveller who published his *Tour Through the Whole Island of Great Britain* in 1726, suggested that refugees from the Palatine should be settled here.

In 1709, ten thousand refugees from the Rhenish Palatinate came to England to escape the miseries of war and oppression in their own country. They were housed in huts on the heaths near London. Some went abroad to found a settlement in Pennsylvania, but the only rational plan for their care was proposed by Defoe. He suggested that certain selected families should be given areas of barren land — like this part of the Forest — so that they would employ others and that in time communities would be formed with churches, schools and shops. Defoe's far-sighted plans even included a health service! It was a splendid plan, like so many of Defoe's economic theories, but came to nothing as Lord Treasurer Godolphin who approved of it, soon lost his office.

When the path divides keep on straight ahead — ignore the path leading a little left downhill. Our path now follows a ridge. You will see the ground falling away forty yards or so over on your left. When the path divides keep straight on (left-hand track). The path becomes a wide greenway, fenced at both sides leading between new beech woods sheltered by pine 'nurses'. When you come to a gravel track, turn left and go through a gate. Here you find another of the Forest's hidden secrets! Standing each side of the track ahead are magnificent Douglas Firs, their tall soaring trunks a rough, flaking reddish-brown and their great sweeping branches sighing in every breath of wind. Douglas Firs, natives of the west of North America, grow very well in the Forest. They are named after David Douglas, a gardener who sent seed over to Britain in 1827.

From the gate, walk between these wonderful trees along the edge of Shave Green Inclosure. When the gravel track turns right and left, keep straight on down the grassy path ahead following the line of the Douglas Firs. You come to a plantation of young pines on the left with several deer hides.

Deer love to browse on young pines and sure enough two deer ran out of it and over my path. I was interested to see they were red deer hinds, not numerous in the Forest. Dark red-brown in colour, not as graceful as the roe and without the fallow's distinctive white patch, their chief beauty is I think their small, daintily-formed heads. Their large prominent ears flopped as they ran back into cover.

Go straight over the next crosstrack and walk on to a gate. Go through the gate and straight on to the foot of a hill covered in oaks and beeches immediately ahead of you. (We are aiming for the minor road which runs in front of Castle Malwood towards Minstead, past Hungerford car park along the top of the hill ahead.) At the foot of the hill follow the track as it bears left along the hillside. Soon you come to a small open grassy area on your left. Do not keep straight on here, but follow our track as it turns right uphill. The track becomes indistinct but continue uphill for about a hundred yards. Then follow the track as it bears left for about thirty yards. Now our path becomes clearer and turns right, uphill again, to meet the minor road by a Forestry Commission barrier. (Do not worry if you lose the path — just walk up the hill and you will come to the minor road.)

Turn left and walk a few yards down the road to Hungerford car park which is on your right. To catch the bus back to Southampton, retrace your steps across the car park to the Minstead road. Turn right for the A31. Cross the westbound carriageway and follow the footpath over the central reservation. You will see the bus stop on the other side of the eastbound carriageway a few yards to your right.

Our second walk begins from the Rufus Stone. If you arrived on the bus, turn left after crossing the A31 and in a few yards turn right down the lane signposted 'The Rufus Stone'. At the foot of the hill you will see the Rufus Stone on your left and the car park on your right where we begin our walk.

By car, drive back from Hungerford car park the way you came to the A31. Turn left along the main road for just a few yards then right over the central reservation for the Rufus Stone. Turn right to follow the eastbound carriageway for a few yards then left down the lane to the Rufus Stone. At the foot of the hill turn into the car park.

Before we begin our walk cross the minor road to look at the Rufus Stone. It looks rather like an iron-encased trig point, shaped like a small tower with four sides. On one side we read 'Here stood the oak tree on which an arrow shot by Sir Walter Tyrrel at a stag glanced and struck King William II, surnamed Rufus, on the breast of which he instantly died on the second day of August Anno 1100.' This most detested of Kings was left where he fell to be found by a charcoal burner called Purkiss who took his body on his cart to Winchester along a route still called the King's road.

According to the contemporary chroniclers William Rufus, now King, was hunting with his younger brother Henry, his good friend Fitzhamon, and Walter Tyrrel who had just arrived from Normandy where the King's enemies had been outlawed. As the sun was setting the King found himself alone with Tyrrel. A stag bounded past. 'Shoot!' cried the King, when his arrow only slightly wounded it. Tyrrel shot and his arrow pierced Rufus's heart. He died immediately. Tyrrel fled to Normandy, but no pursuit was organised. Henry made straight to Winchester where he secured the national treasury, then continued to London where he persuaded the Bishop to crown him King on 5 August — only three days after his brother's death! Haste was necessary as Henry had another brother, Duke Robert, to whom he had promised allegiance, but who happened to be conveniently in Normandy at the time. Fitzhamon, the fourth member of the hunting party, loyally rushed to Normandy to tell Robert what had happened.

If it was murder, you can take your pick among a host of suspects. The Saxons hated their Norman Kings of course but even his own countrymen detested Rufus. The clergy, rich and powerful, objected to his choice of favourites, the barons disliked him for extending his Forest Laws over their lands. Then there were the allies of his brothers who had their eyes on the crown. They were not the sons of William the Conqueror for nothing! Evidence does seem to point to Henry as being the villain of the piece. If you would like to pursue this remarkable whodunit further you should read Duncan Grinnel Milne's book *The Killing of William Rufus*. Tyrrel protested he was innocent even on his deathbed!

Return to the minor road and cross over to the car park. On your left you will see a little track and a sign 'Access to Cottage, please keep clear'. Follow this towards a real New Forest cottage with a charming old world garden; the sort of cottage I felt could well be haunted by the ghost dog of the Forest. He was Walter Tyrrel's dog and is able to rush in and out of houses through the walls! He was a much more effective threat for naughty Forest children than 'Boney'!

Turn right in front of the cottage and walk on with the hedge close beside you on your left. The hedge merges into the Inclosure boundary — an embankment sometimes surmounted with a fence. Keep straight on into the woods, keeping the Inclosure boundary a few yards away on your left. Use the boundary as your guide as you walk on, over a more open area then down to cross a stream. As you climb the opposite bank, with the boundary now very close on your left, you will see the fields of the tiny Forest hamlet of Lower Canterton just beyond. The embankment becomes a hedge and now using the hedge as your guide follow it round as it curves left with the open Forest on your right and the scattered houses on your left. Soon you join a gravel track. Follow this straight ahead.

Dreaming peacefully beneath the shelter of the Forest oaks, this part of Canterton looks as remote as it was in the days of William Rufus. The name 'Canterton' (meaning 'the village of the Kentish men' or the Jutes) recalls that it was Jutish tribes who first settled in the New Forest after the departure of the Roman legions.

Ahead you will glimpse a large white house. Look for a wide green way leading left between the cottages. There is a bridleway sign on your right but this is partly obscured by brambles. This is a right of way leading to Piper's Copse. Follow the path left, down to a stream and into the copse. The track through the trees has sunk between high banks entwined with tree roots which make such perfect homes for wild flowers. The path leads to a lane which meets a minor road. Turn left here and follow the minor road towards Upper Canterton. You pass the Walter Tyrrel Inn on the left. Continue along the road — or past the cottage — to the Rufus Stone car park.

To catch the bus retrace your steps up the hill to the A31. The bus stop for Southampton is on your left.

• THE NORTHERN FOREST

This is the wildest and most remote part of the Forest. You will find some old woods here — the great beeches in Bramshaw Woods can rival those in Denny — but generally the country is more open and hilly. Several streams run across the northern Forest south-west to the Avon through shallow valleys. Each valley is different and provides splendid walks along the streamsides and in the bordering Inclosures. The streams here run clear and sparkling over gravel quite unlike the reddish-brown brooks of the central area. Dockens Water which I describe in *New Forest Walks* is perhaps the best known. It is easily reached from Fritham. But my favourite valley runs a little further south threaded by the Linford brook.

Walk 19

THE LINFORD VALLEY

Starting point: Linford Valley car park. Bus: Forest Corner, 3 miles east of Ringwood, off A31.

Distance: 4 miles. The walk to and from the bus stop will add two extra miles

The Linford Valley is one of the most bewitching of the many surprises the Forest holds for the explorer. Our walk takes us along the valley of the Linford brook through very old woodlands to climb up to a hill fort and the open heath at King's Garden before returning down the other side of the Linford valley. The distance is about four miles if you start from the car park. It is two miles more if you start from Forest Corner.

Our starting point is the car park at the western end of the Linford valley, three miles north of Ringwood, just within the western boundary of the Forest. From the Cadnam roundabout, drive west along the A31 towards Ringwood. Continue past Picket Post, where you will pass a turning to Burley on the left. After about three quarters of a mile, turn right down a minor road signposted North Poulner. (It is on the crest of the hill.) If you are arriving by bus from Southampton or Ringwood alight at Forest Corner close to the turning for North Poulner. Drive

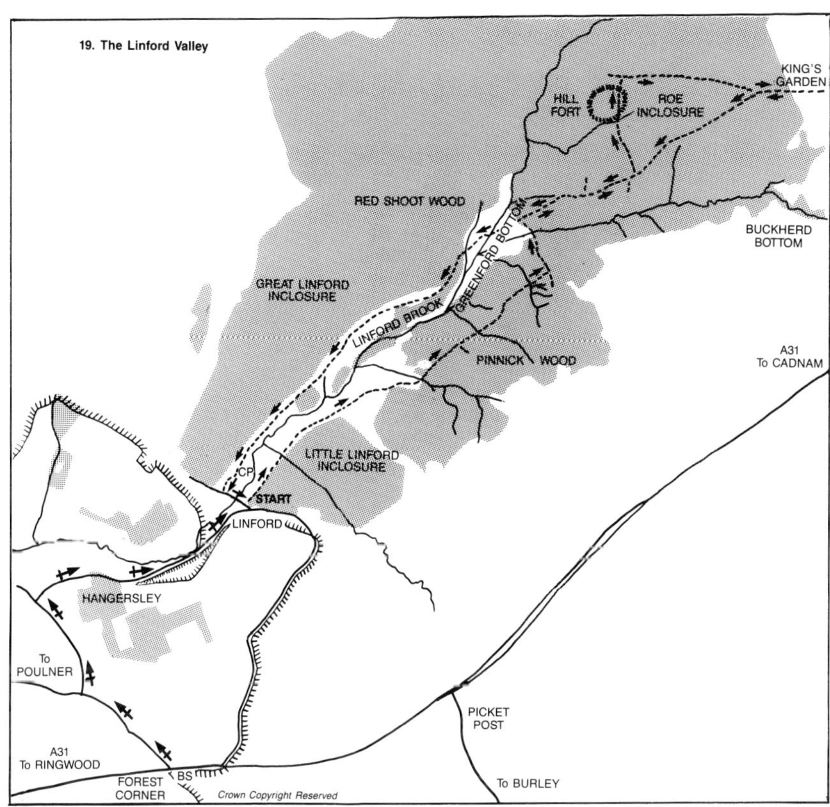

Additions to Key:
CP *Linford Valley car park*
For general Key see p. viii

or walk down the lane and at the first road junction turn right for Hangersley and North Poulner. At the next crossroads turn right following the sign for Linford. Now you are following a country lane down a prettily wooded valley. After about half a mile, at the next road junction, turn left, cross the bridge over the Linford brook, and follow the track which bears right to the parking areas.

We begin our walk along the right-hand side of the stream as you look up the valley. So from the car park walk back to the road, turn left and cross the stream, and you will see a green path on the left running along the hillside beside Little Linford Inclosure. Turn left past the barrier and follow this path with the stream on your left and the Inclosure on your right. At the end of the Inclosure you come to a small open heath. Follow the green track as it leads at first straight ahead then bears slightly right towards Pinnick Wood. With the trees now close on your right, cross a bridge over a small stream and walk straight ahead into Pinnick Wood itself.

Pinnick sounds delightful, and it is. You will find it a glorious tangle of old oaks twisted about with ivy and honeysuckle and half-smothered with enormous hollies. Some of the hoary oak tree branches bend so low that they touch the ground and seem to be supporting the main trunk. Young seedlings spring up everywhere protected as they are by these dense thickets of blackthorn, brambles and holly.

When the path divides keep straight on along the main track (the one to the left). This leads you out of the wood to the open heath of Greenford Bottom near Roe Inclosure. A little way over the heath on your left you will see a gravel track which we aim to join close to Roe Inclosure. So do not cross to it yet but walk on up the valley keeping the woods on your right. Walk through a more thickly wooded area to meet a green path. Turn left to cross a bridge over a stream and a few yards further on you come to the gravel track I mentioned earlier.

Turn right and follow this track through the gate ahead into Roe Inclosure. Although this is mainly a pine wood, and has not been left to its own devices like Pinnick, the path is fringed with beautiful sweet chestnut trees, their elegant leaves like long tapering fingers.

Our path leads uphill and over the remains of an Iron Age hill fort. As you climb, ignore a wide path on the left. When you are almost at the top you reach a crosstrack. Turn left here along a green ride which leads you over the outer embankment of the fort. Cross the level ground in the centre and follow the green way over the other embankment and walk on until you come to a gravelled track. Turn right and follow this track east for about three-quarters of a mile. This brings you to a gate and out onto the open heath at King's Garden. Here, in contrast to the old woods we have explored so far, rolling heathlands spread before us. To the left the horizon is bounded by the dark line of the pinewoods of Milkham Inclosure where the Linford brook rises, to the right are Bratley Plain and Buckherd Bottom dotted with trees and scored with shallow valleys.

As the last name suggests, this should be a good place for deer spotting. And when we were here we were lucky. There they were — graceful dark brown shapes gliding through the trees. White patches on their rumps showed they were fallow. They had no fear of us so I had no opportunity to test the truth of a story I have been told. Evidently it is the does who guard the herd when threatened, forming a defensive ring around the bucks. When running for cover, the does run on the outside and part when they reach the shelter of the trees to let the bucks escape first.

Return to the gate at King's Garden and retrace your steps for a short distance to take the first turning on your left down a gravel track. This is our way back through Roe Inclosure.

Continue down the hill to rejoin the track you previously left to look at the hill fort. This brings you down to the gate out of Roe Wood at the head of the Linford valley. Go through the gate and follow the gravel track ahead over the open glade between Redshoot Wood and Pinnick Wood.

This glade is Greenford Bottom where you will see the remains of 'bee-gardens'. There are several of these in the Forest: small, embanked rectangular areas, the relics of a custom followed by local bee-keepers a hundred years ago. Hives were sent to the Forest, which is still famous for its honey, to be looked after by the foresters who kept them in these bee-gardens, secure from disturbance by animals. Every New Forest cottager had his hives which were vital to provide the family with a cheap means of sweetening their food and the essential ingredient of mead which was brewed for special occasions. So valued were the bees that if there was a death in the family the bees had to be told about it. If it was the master of the house who had died, each hive had to be tapped three times. If these precautions were not taken, the bees — or brownies as they are known locally — would be upset and either die or disappear.

Across Greenford Bottom you come back to the Linford brook. Cross the stream by the wooden footbridge and walk over the valley towards a gate leading into Redshoot Wood. Do not enter the wood but turn left just before the gate to follow the path that wanders down the valley back to the car park. Go through a small wood then over wide glades with the wood on your right and the stream on your left. If you prefer, you can follow the small winding path along the bank of the stream; both ways are beautiful. Last time we took the wide path along the edge of the wood. Beneath the fence in several places the grass is worn away from the top of the inclosure embankment and shows clearly the broad five-toed footprints of badgers. At night they must come out of the wood to feed and drink in the stream. Several very fine oaks stand like sentinels along this path. I noticed one with a beautiful shawl of ferns draped over the top of the main trunk and hanging over its branches. The way brings you straight back to the Linford car park. If you came by bus turn left over the bridge, then turn right to retrace your route back to the stop at Forest Corner.

Walk 20

FRITHAM AND EYEWORTH

Starting point: Fritham car park, just past the Royal Oak Inn. Bus: Fritham, the Royal Oak.

Distance 4½ miles.

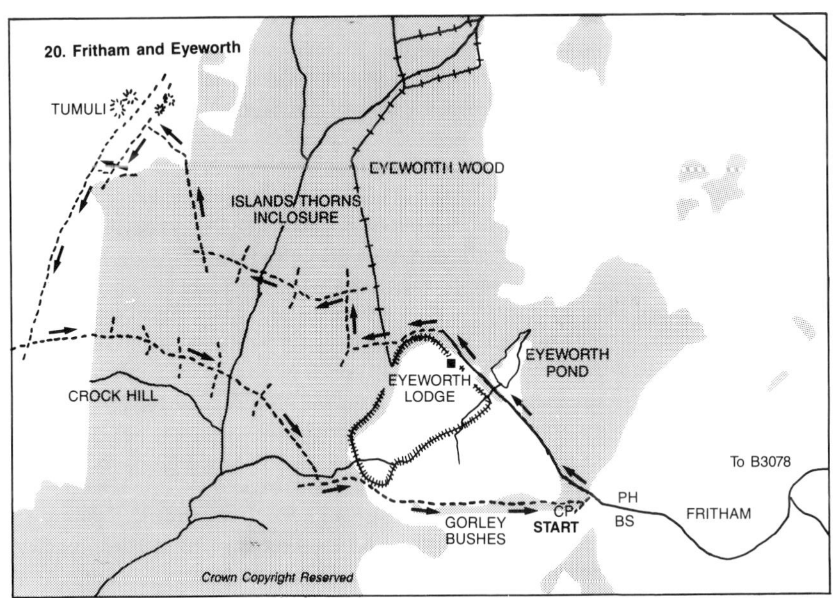

Additions to Key:
CP Fritham car park   PH Royal Oak Inn   +++ Fenced embankment
For general key see p. viii

Fritham is a scattering of houses and farms in the most remote part of the Forest. It is a marvellous centre for walking and several good paths lead from the car park where we begin our walk, just past the Royal Oak Inn. There is a bus service to Fritham and the stop is outside the Royal Oak. The easiest way to reach Fritham by car is to take the minor road, B3079 for Brook and Bramshaw, at the Cadnam roundabout. Just past the Bell Inn in Brook, follow the B3078 for Fordingbridge. After about a mile and a half, turn left for Fritham. The second turning on your right leads you through the village — spreading over the countryside like all Forest villages — and eventually brings you to the Royal Oak on your right. Drive on into the car park just beyond the Inn.

To begin our walk we follow the metalled lane leading from the car park downhill to Eyeworth. Leave the Royal Oak on your right and keep straight on across the green with the car park on your left. As you reach the top of the hill, beside the track which leads left into the parking area, look for an old, black iron postbox. This is the clue to the whole nature of this part of the Forest! Nowhere could look more peaceful and serene than the glades of oak, beech and holly that surround you but once this was the centre of a thriving industry. During the nineteenth century the Schultze gunpowder works flourished at Eyeworth in the valley just ahead of us. The postbox, which was renovated by the Forestry Commission in 1976, was placed here to save the postman part of his journey. He delivered and collected letters every day except Sundays. Postage was one penny for a letter and a halfpenny for a newspaper.

Follow the lane down the hill and now this delectable little valley opens before you. Eyeworth Pond sparkles through the trees a little to your right and a cloud of oaks and beeches clothes the hillside beyond. Follow the lane down to the water. Today Eyeworth Pond is an idyllic spot with flotillas of ducks paddling about carpets of waterlilies. It must have been very different when the gunpowder works stood here! The stream was dammed to make the present pond for cooling purposes and a whole factory complex was built with huts for the workmen. The firm pro-duced sporting powder used in the shooting of game, hares and rabbits. Old inhabitants of Fritham will describe those days still when men came to work here from as far as Downton, Redlynch and Fordingbridge. I was shown a brochure published by the works in 1865, showing the extent of the buildings and the various processes involved and the whole concern was extensive and prosperous. The works were closed in 1910 when the last of the original three leases expired.

The valley is the perfect site for a village but where is Eyeworth? The name is derived from the Saxon name 'Ivare', 'a wooded hill', and the settlement was important enough to be mentioned in the *Domesday Book*. Some historians believe that this was one of the Saxon villages William the Conqueror destroyed to make his hunting forest. By the time of Henry III the Forest laws were paramount but a certain Roger Beteston was allowed to hold some land here at Eyeworth on condition he entertained the King on his hunting expeditions.

Follow the lane straight on to cross the stream and pass Eyeworth Lodge (the manager's house when the gunpowder works were open) on your left. The lane climbs to Eyeworth Wood. Keep straight on past the Forestry Commission barrier keeping a fenced embankment close on your left. Follow the fence round as it curves left. You come to a corner as the fence turns sharply left. Do not follow it but walk straight ahead (your back is to the fence) for just a few yards. (There is no path at this point.) Cross a well-marked inclosure embankment immediately ahead — the path is clear now leading over a worn part of the boundary — and follow a beautiful woodland path straight ahead. As you walk along this terraced path you look left downhill through glades of young beech trees. There are very few old trees here as possibly they were burnt to make charcoal for the gunpowder.

When you come to a wide crosstrack, turn right and follow the track uphill with an inclosure fence on your left. Most of the woodland tracks we follow now are wide and embanked, constructed to carry laden wagons safely. At the top of the hill you come to a gate leading to an open area at the approach to Islands Thorns Inclosure. Go through the gate. Turn left along the grassy path which leads down through the trees, bearing a little right to take you over a crosstrack and down to a stream. Cross the stream and keep on over the next crosstrack. Continue uphill, and at the next crosstrack turn right. Walk up to a gate opening out of the Inclosure onto the heath.

Go through the gate and there is a different world! The heath rolls away to the north-west with the blue curve of the Wiltshire Downs on the horizon. Keep straight ahead from the gate along a rather indistinct track over the heath. A line of old burial mounds, or tumuli, stretches ahead of you. As you reach the mounds you come to a clear crossing track. Oddly, this pattern is repeated. Over the heath ahead you will see another line of tumuli beside another track. This is the track we eventually follow but as there is no path to it at this point, turn left along the first crosstrack. Soon you come to a crosstrack — Islands Thorns Inclosure boundary is over the heath on your left. Turn right to walk the few yards to meet the good track I mentioned. Turn left and follow this grass and gravel track over the heath. After about half a mile you come to a crosstrack. Turn left towards the Inclosure again. Follow the track into the Inclosure. Our way now is straight ahead along a wide embanked ride. Pass a turning on your left and keep straight on past two joining tracks.

On your right is Crock Hill. As the name suggests, this was the site of a pottery that flourished here for several hundred years while the Romans ruled Britain. Banks and mounds mark the site of the community. Excavating here, John Wise found the remains of three or four kilns. A typical kiln was about twelve feet in diameter and was constructed of puddled clay. Inside was a combustion chamber where wood or charcoal was burnt with the aid of suitably arranged flues and an upper dome where the pottery was arranged to be fired. John Wise found parts of oil flasks, strainers, funnels, part of a lamp and, most fascinating, some of the workmen's tools that had been accidentally dropped into the furnace but were still recognizable. Most of the pottery he found was slate-coloured, grey or a faint yellow. You can still find fragments of pottery which covered a wide range of bowls, platters and flagons, often decorated with a linked design. From coins found near the kilns it is believed these kilns ceased production about AD380 as the Roman legions were being withdrawn.

Keep straight on over a crosstrack to cross a bridge over a stream. We go over another crosstrack and then uphill. Cross another stream and you come to a wide gravel T-junction. Turn left and follow this wide gravelled way as it bears a little right past green fields on your left. In the field you will see one of the mounds where the gunpowder was stored. Our track winds uphill through some magnificent pollarded oaks to Fritham car park, in front of the green opposite the Royal Oak.

Walk 21

NOMANSLAND TO PIPER'S WAIT
AND BRAMSHAW CHURCH

Starting point: The Lamb Inn, Nomansland. Bus: the Lamb Inn.

Distance: 3 miles. The walk to Bramshaw Church will add an extra mile.

Campsite: Piper's Wait.

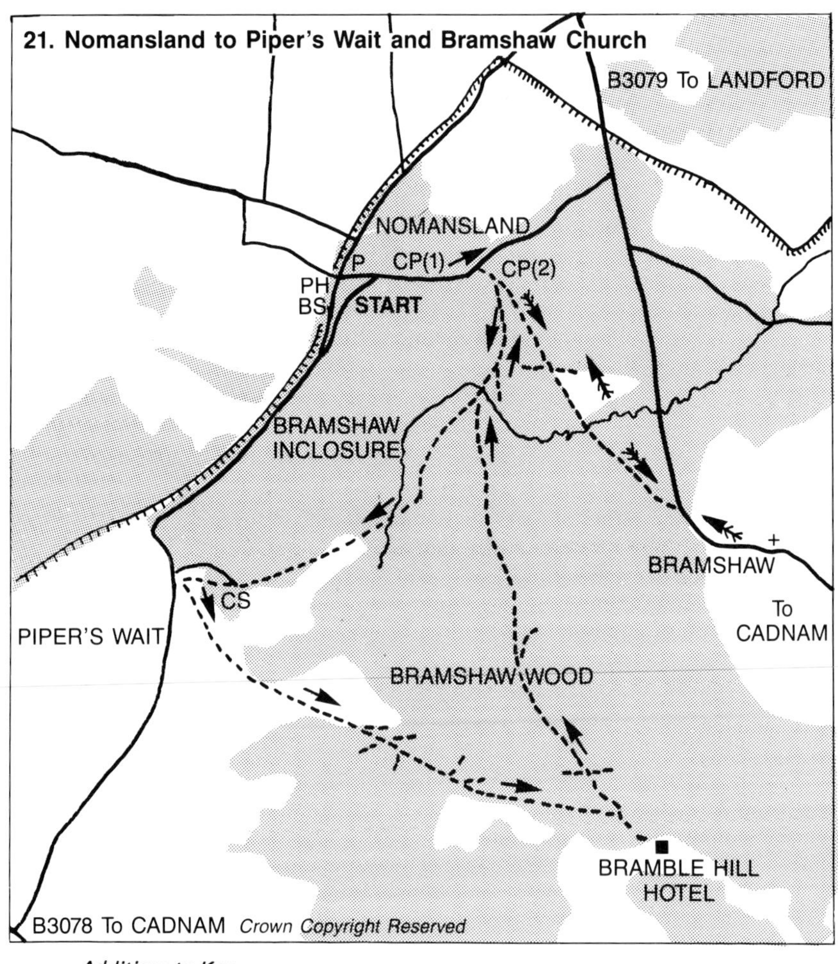

Additions to Key:

PH	*Lamb Inn*	CS	*Piper's Wait campsite*
P	*Parking*	◀ *Route to Bramshaw Church*	
CP(1)	*Nomansland Green car park*		
CP(2)	*Bramshaw Wood car park*	*For general Key see p. viii*	

So much of the delight of the Forest lies in what Robert Browning called 'the shapes of things, their colours, lights and shades, changes, surprises. . . .' The moors, woods, plains and valleys are so full of contrasts and always changing with the weather and the seasons. But the most striking contrast is between the Forest and the countryside around it. No one needs notices, fences or cattle grids to let him know he is crossing the Forest boundary; the Forest looks, and feels, entirely different.

This walk takes you to the northern boundary of the Forest where oak and beech woods confront the rolling Wiltshire Downs. Our starting point is the attractive, if oddly-named, village of Nomansland. The three-mile ramble from the village takes us to the highest point in the Forest at Piper's Wait and I suggest another short walk to Bramshaw Church.

There is a small informal campsite at Piper's Wait which makes an alternative starting point. I will indicate when to join the walk from the campsite in the text.

Our walk begins from the Lamb Inn in Nomansland. Buses stop outside. Driving along the A336 from Southampton to Cadnam take the B3078 for Fordingbridge. In Brook follow the road right — the B3079 — signposted Landford. Go through Bramshaw and past a turning on the right to Newbridge. Just before a cattle grid you will see a minor road on the left signposted Nomansland. (Two lanes merge around a grassy triangle.) You pass Bramshaw Wood car park on your left then Nomansland Green car park on your right. Keep straight on in the direction of the road running in front of the Lamb Inn. There is a parking area on your right before you come to the minor road. If this is full, park in either of the two car parks on the way.

Nomansland is a fascinating village. The main street wanders along the Forest — and incidentally the county — boundary so that the single row of houses stand facing the Forest with their backs to the downs. The Lamb Inn is in Wiltshire except for its front step which is in Hampshire! Inside the inn we discovered how Nomansland came to have its strange name, more reminiscent of a battlefield than a peaceful Forest village. From a newspaper article framed over the fireplace we discovered that until 1800 Nomansland was something of a battlefield. If anyone tried to apply New Forest squatter's rights and build a house here, the authorities pulled it down. No one was certain whether the land was within the Forest or not. In 1800 the New Forest Commissioners decided to allow people to build and in 1841 there were thirty-two houses and a population of one hundred and forty-nine. H M Lievens, writing in *The Salisbury Times* in 1910, tells a more romantic story. He says the village was founded by a gypsy in the eighteenth century who was later joined by two or three other young unmarried men. They wooed brides from neighbouring villages to join them in their landlordless paradise. Whatever the explanation, they were a very independent community. When the first county rates were levied in the mid-nineteenth century, the collector for Nomansland was too terrified to do his job, so he paid the whole six shillings and six pence from his own pocket. Later when this timid soul sent his daughter to try and recoup his losses she was met by a torrent of abuse from one cottager who was asked to contribute a penny farthing.

Walk back along the minor road opposite the Lamb Inn over the green. You pass Nomansland Well of Sacrifice on your left, a memorial to the fallen in both world wars built over the site of the original village well. Follow the road straight ahead into Bramshaw Wood beneath fine beech trees. Pass Nomansland Green car park on your left and a little further on you come to Bramshaw Wood car park on your right. Turn right along the gravel track leading to the parking area and walk straight ahead over the car park. On the other side of the gravelled area you will see the corner of the embankment marking the inclosure boundary and two paths which meet just in front of you. We take the right-hand path to begin our walk which runs to the left of the embankment fairly steeply downhill. When the path divides keep straight on (right-hand path) downhill to cross a small stream. Another path joins our way here from the left which is our return route but now we keep straight ahead. The inclosure embankment runs beside us almost the whole way to Piper's Wait.

As you walk down the valley, slopes planted with young oaks and beeches rise on either side. Here and there is the massive form of a much older tree which has survived from earlier times. These beautiful woods were famous as early as the thirteenth century when they provided the timber used in building Salisbury Cathedral. They were one of the last refuges of the gypsies. When they were married in Bramshaw Church, the gypsies were described evocatively as being 'of the Forest'. The woods provided shelter for gangs of smugglers who flourished in these parts. There is a story that one Nomansland gang concealed a hundred pounds' worth of brandy in forty kegs in a barn at Cadnam. Home they went, happily unaware they had been seen. When they returned to collect their haul, they found nothing. Their unnoticed observer had helped himself to the lot! So disgusted were the Nomansland gang that they disbanded on the spot.

Cross another stream in a deep gully and walk on still keeping the inclosure boundary on your right. Soon the track begins to climb and bears a little left away from the boundary. Ancient oaks spread lichen-covered branches overhead. Follow the track as it now bears a little right to the highest point of the hillside. Walk past the great oaks and beeches that crown the ridge and past a barrier which brings you out on the heath at Piper's Wait.

(If you are camping at Piper's Wait you can join the circular walk at this point.)

Follow the gravel track from the site towards a minor road and a barrier. The hill you see directly ahead is Piper's Wait, the highest point in the New Forest, 422 feet above sea level. Just before you come to the road you will see a green track (gravel beneath) leading left, south east, over the heath. Turn left and follow this path as it leads you towards the crest of the valley. The dense line of Bramshaw woods falls away to give a wonderful view of the wide valley backed by folds of massed woodlands fading into the soft blue haze of the downs. When the path divides bear right and go straight over the next crosstrack. Take the left hand of the two tracks ahead. You pass a green path to the left and our path divides. Keep straight on (the right-hand path). This soon bears left and becomes a better gravelled track leading downhill through magnificent woodlands. At the foot of the hill you will see the redbrick stables of Bramble Hill Hotel. This is built on the site of an old hunting lodge and part of the older building can still be traced. A small path leads to the gate into the stables. Do not follow this but turn left — due north — slightly uphill, bearing a little left to meet a green crosstrack. Go straight over and walk up a shallow gully directly ahead. Climb over the rise at the end of the gully and now as you drop down the other side a beautiful woodland way lies in front of you. When the path divides walk straight on (left-hand path) along the main path through Bramshaw Wood to join the path on which we began our walk just before the little stream. Retrace your way uphill to Bramshaw Wood car park.

Before returning to the village you might like to look at Bramshaw Church. It is a lovely walk of about a mile. There are several tracks from Bramshaw Wood car park and it is important to find the right one! From the car park take only a few steps along our original track leading to Piper's Wait. Now you will see a less distinct path leading left. Turn left and follow this, straight over a crosstrack and downhill. It is a lovely path shaded by oaks and beeches and leading through glades full of wild flowers. Keep straight on over all crosstracks down to a shallow valley threaded by a little stream. Go over the bridge and follow the path through the woods which brings you to a barrier by the minor road between Bramshaw and Landford, the B3079. Turn right and follow the road uphill to Bramshaw Church.

Once there may have been a Saxon building here, but the earliest part of the present church is the north wall built during the twelfth century. The vicar, the Rev. Ben Elliott, has written a most interesting booklet full of New Forest stories which you will find inside the church. I particularly enjoyed this snippet taken from the Bramshaw Church records: 'Resolution of the Vestry, April 27th, 1827, that Mrs Jones and Mrs Marshall shall take care of the church as before and that they shall confine their pigs during the hours of Service.'

Retrace the same route back to Bramshaw Wood car park and Nomansland village.

Walk 22

GODSHILL INCLOSURE AND WOODGREEN

Starting point: Deadman Hill car park, off B3078. Bus: Woodgreen.

Distance: 6 miles.
From Woodgreen: 4½ miles.

The western boundary of the Forest today lies along the valley of the river Avon. To the north, above Woodgreen, the Forest trees edge a cliff which gives marvellous views over the river to Breamore and the farmlands and downs beyond. This walk takes us to Woodgreen and then along the cliff to explore the most impressive Iron Age hill fort in the Forest, high above the Avon at Godshill.

You can start this walk from Woodgreen, in which case the distance round is about four and a half miles, or from the small car park at Deadman Hill, near Godshill, which make a longer ramble of about six miles. I will describe the longer walk and indicate where to join the circle for the shorter one. To reach Deadman Hill car park, take the B3078 (Fordingbridge) road from the Cadnam roundabout. After you pass the junction with the B3080, continue for about two miles in the direction of Godshill. You will see the sign for Deadman Hill car park on your right. If you look at the new Ordnance Survey map for the area, Deadman Hill car park is at the point on the B3078 where the road bends south for Godshill, just above the 100-metre contour mark. The car park, by the way, is a far nicer place than its name suggests!

With your back to the road, follow the track which leads north past a barrier downhill from the car park. At your feet is the wide heather-covered valley of the Millersford Brook. Crowning the skyline to the left is Godshill Inclosure with its lovely mixed woods of oaks, beeches, pines and sweet chestnuts through which

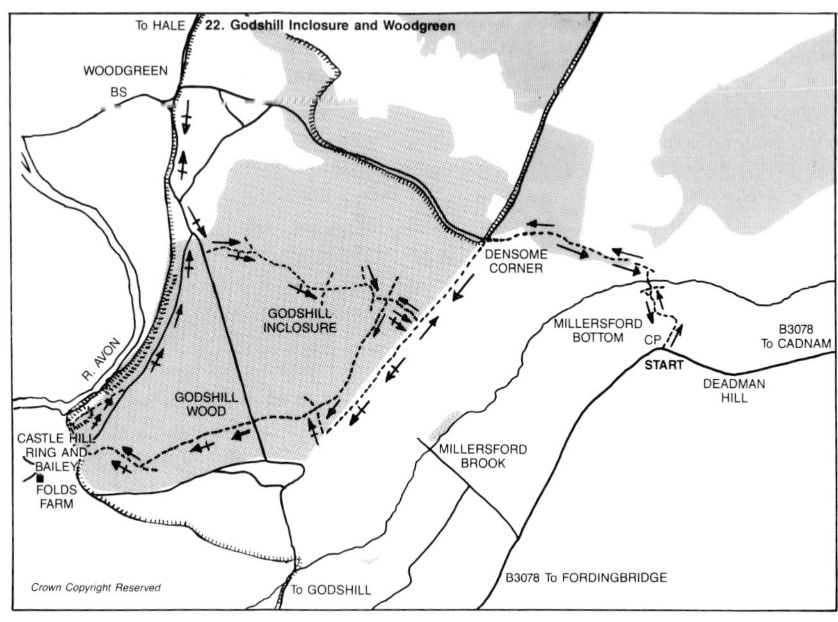

Addition to Key:
CP *Deadman Hill car park*
For general Key see p. viii

---

our way lies. The track bears left towards a conspicuous grove of dark Scots pines then turns right to lead downhill towards a stream. When the path divides bear a little right for a few yards, over a crossing track, then walk straight ahead to the stream. Cross the stream. Our way is up the hillside ahead to join a minor road at Densome Corner beside Godshill Inclosure. There is a good track all the way but unfortunately it has become overgrown in places at first. With your back to the stream look a little to your right and you will see an embankment and fence which is immediately to the right of the path we want to follow. Cross the green lawns ahead and make your way uphill, picking up the good track by the embankment when you can. You may have to bear left to skirt the bushes at first. Follow what soon becomes an excellent track to Densome Corner on a minor road running from Hale to Woodgreen.

Now take the path immediately on your left which runs along the side of the valley with the south-east edge of Godshill Inclosure on your right. Walk across the green lawns along the hillside to a gate leading right into the woods. Turn right, through the gate and follow the track until you meet a gravelled way. Turn left here to follow a pleasant path shaded by sweet chestnuts, oaks and pines.

When you come to a crosstrack keep straight on. (If you start this walk at Woodgreen this is your half-way point and you join the route by the track coming in from the left at this crossways. Follow the way I describe from here and I will complete the circle at the end.)

Walk through the pines to a gate which brings you to a road crossing the Inclosure from Woodgreen to Godshill. Go over the road and enter the Inclosure again through the opposite gate. Follow the gravel track ahead through more varied woodland. Just after a joining track on the left our path curves round to the right and drops steeply downhill to bear left to a gate. Go through the gate out of the Inclosure on to another minor road running between Godshill and Woodgreen. Across the green lawn ahead is Folds Farm whose venerable walls still show traces of the important manor it was in medieval times.

Turn right on to the road and you will see a wide green path leading steeply up the hill to your left. It is steep but short! Climb up this path, go over a gravelled track and keep straight ahead over an embankment. Cross another gravel track and bear a little right over more of the high, rounded embankments of Castle Hill Iron Age fort. Soon you are standing on the smooth green lawn that forms the central area of this wonderful fort. You are encircled by earth walls and ditches still clearly visible. This is an exciting place — full of atmosphere. It is easy to imagine the Celtic tribesmen standing here over two thousand years ago and deciding that this sheer cliff, high above a great silver loop of the Avon, would be an ideal defensive position. They built many such forts, crowning the embankments with timber ramparts enclosing stockades with strong wooden gates. They were an artistic as well as warlike people as their pottery and intricately-patterned jewellery prove.

Walk across the central area of the fort to where you can look down the cliff to the Avon on your left. With the valley on your left, walk from the fort through the trees, north, in the direction of Woodgreen. From the many outlines of ditches and entrenchments I would guess quite a large village once thrived here in the shelter of the fort. Soon you leave the trees to continue along the minor road running along the top of the escarpment to Woodgreen. All the way the views of the valley are lovely with the Avon curving through lush meadows past old mills and mellowed brick cottages. The village, tucked in an arm of the river, clustered around its Saxon church and overlooked by an Elizabethan manor house, is Breamore.

You come to a road junction, left for Woodgreen village and right for Godshill. Our way is right here, but you might like to explore the village first. Woodgreen is an interesting village, clinging to the hillside above the Avon and just within the Forest boundary. In the surrounding orchards you can still see the village's famous 'Merry Trees'. These are a special kind of black cherry, sweet and juicy. Once, when the trees were ready to harvest, folk came from far and wide to pick them and enjoy what were known as 'Merry Sundays'. As it says in *It Happened in Hampshire,* in order to keep the birds from getting the fruit first, the residents used to hang tins from the branches with chains suspended inside to rattle. Ropes were attached and led through windows so they could be pulled from bed early in the morning. But the merry Sundays evidently became a little *too* merry. Finally a clergyman was so shocked by the proceedings that he stopped the custom. But the trees still flourish.

And Woodgreen has a unique treasure. If you would like to see what life here was like in 1933, visit the village hall. In that year, two young artists, Robert Baker and Ted Payne, covered all the available wall space with scenes of Woodgreen, using the villagers as models. It is therefore a wonderfully life-like and authentic record. George Brewer is up a ladder picking apples, Miss Tazwell climbs the hill with her goats, the Misses Davies arrange flower vases at the flower show, and the boys and girls attend Sunday School looking their starched and shining best.

From Woodgreen walk back up the Godshill road, past the turning to Castle Hill which was the point where we made a detour from our route to explore the village. (If you start this walk from Woodgreen come this way, up the Godshill Road to join the longer walk.) A few yards past the Castle Hill turning, you will see a gate leading into Godshill Inclosure on the left. Go through the gate and follow the path ahead which soon meets a better track. Keep on along this good track as it bears right. Follow it over all crosstracks, until you come to a T-junction. Turn right here along the gravel for a few yards, then take the little green path leading left. We are now back on our original route which takes us to the gate on the south-east edge of Godshill Inclosure. Go through the gate and before you is the Millersford valley with Deadman Hill car park on the top of the opposite hillside. From the gate, turn left and retrace your steps to the corner of the Hale–Woodgreen road, then down to the stream and up to the car park, following our path as it bears left through the pines.

To complete the circle, if you began this walk at Woodgreen, turn right from the gate leading out of Godshill Inclosure and walk along the straight path along the edge of the wood. Soon you will come to another gate into the Inclosure. Go through it and follow the track for a short distance. When you come to a crosstrack turn left. You are now on the route to Castle Hill at the point I described as being about half-way in your walk.

Walk 23

STONEY CROSS AND BUSHY BRATLEY

Starting point: Andrews Mare car park, Stoney Cross. Bus: Stoney Cross.

Distance: 8 miles.

Campsite: Stoney Cross.

This is one of my favourite walks. It leads you through one of the most magical places in the Forest, the old woods of Bushy Bratley. Take a whole day for this walk if you can.

Our starting point is Stoney Cross which is beside the A31 Cadnam–Ringwood road. Driving from Southampton towards Ringwood, about two miles west of the Cadnam roundabout, a minor road, leading north to Fritham and south to Emery Down and Lyndhurst, crosses the A31. This is Stoney Cross. Turn left as for Emery Down and after about a quarter of a mile follow the car park sign pointing right. Follow the gravel track to the car park which is called Andrews Mare. If you are driving from Ringwood there is no right turn into the Emery Down road so keep on to the Cadnam roundabout and turn there.

Buses stop at Stoney Cross. From the bus stop beside the A31 turn along the Emery Down road and follow the car park sign to begin the walk.

If you are camping at Stoney Cross or Ocknell you are perfectly placed for this

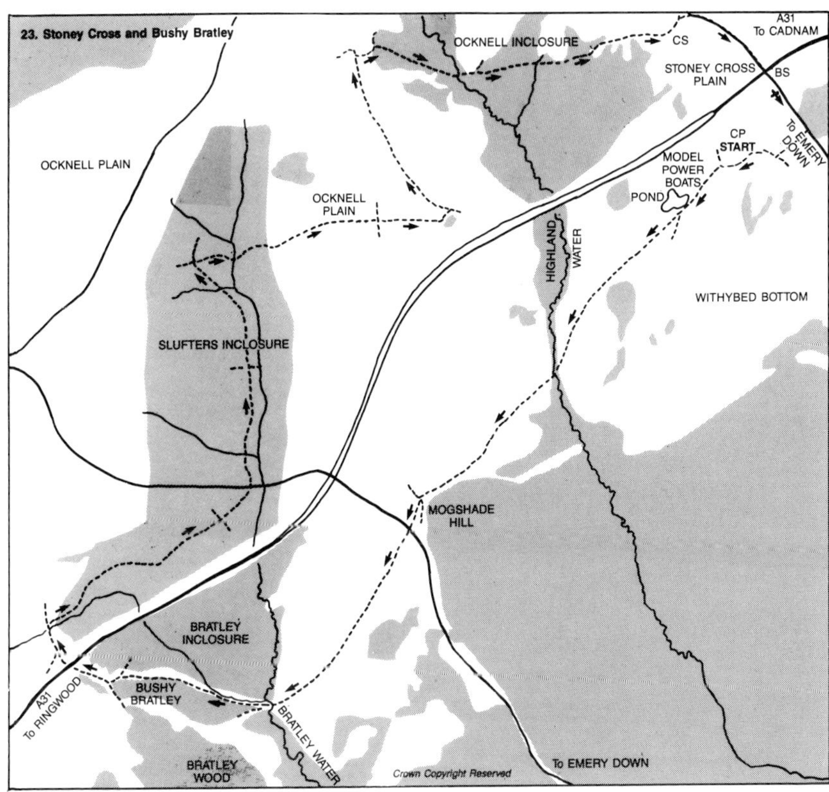

Additions to Key:
CS *Stoney Cross campsite*
CP *Andrew's Mare car park*

For general Key see p. viii

walk. Cross the A31 and follow the Emery Down road to turn right for Andrews Mare car park. The walk returns past the campsite so you will not need to walk back to the car park.

To the left of the sign 'Andrews Mare' you will see a good green path leading west past a Forestry Commission barrier. Follow this wide greenway of soft springing turf. When the path divides bear left. Now you pass a large pond with pleasant shingle beaches. This is sometimes used for sailing model boats. Beyond the water you will see two tracks ahead. Ignore the path bearing left fond keep straight on down the greenway. Soon the heath becomes wilder and more beautiful. The path dips and rises over a series of shallow valleys as it leads towards a long dark line of woods on the horizon. As you leave the trees to the right of an oak wood you come to a low, heath-covered ridge. To the left, the heath slopes down to willow-veiled marshes, called Withybed Bottom. Ahead and round to the right you now see dense masses of woodlands. As we came on to the ridge we were 'buzzed' by swallows! They dived, circled and soared round our heads, their creamy white breasts catching the sunlight, then swooping low they showed us the ink-blue sheen of their backs and wings.

The path leaves the ridge and runs steeply downhill to a stream, Highland Water. The stream is narrow here and usually easy to ford. Cross the stream and walk through its fringe of oaks and hollies to climb the gentle slope ahead. As you reach the top to stand high on the heath once more, you will see the dark pines crowning Mogshade Hill ahead more clearly. Our way lies just to the right of the pines. The view back is lovely too, the Forest's heaths and woods rolling away to the east in all their glory of colour, light and shade. Walk straight on towards the pines of Mogshade and pass them on your left. We aim to carry straight on for Bushy Bratley, but there is a little maze of paths at this point. Immediately after the pines our path meets a crosstrack. Go over it and follow the green path ahead which bears very slightly left. This quickly brings you to a minor road (running south-east to Emery Down). Over the road you will see a most attractive grassy path leading south-west over the heath. Cross the minor road and follow this way which now becomes really beautiful. The path slopes gradually downhill towards Bratley Water. Beyond the stream the hillsides rise shaded with oaks which stand singly revealing all their beauty of form and colour among their green glades. An irregular verge of beeches casts a heavier shadow among the surrounding ferns and heather. This is Bushy Bratley, a venerable wood even for the New Forest.

Cross Bratley Water and after a few yards turn right to follow a green path through Bratley Inclosure. At first, the stream runs fairly close on your right. You walk through silent glades of oak trees along what seemed to us to be a lost valley, a part of England's history where Robin Hood would have felt entirely at home. The huge pollarded trees — I counted ten trunks on one tree twined and twisted together to form a miniature wood of its own — the wild flowers, the spicy smell of gorse and gold withey, make this an enchanted place.

No wonder Charles Kingsley chose Bushy Bratley as the setting of one of his most romantic poems. His 'Ballad of the New Forest' tells the story of a keeper's daughter whose lover was, unfortunately, a deer poacher. She warns him that one day he will be caught by her father and one evening the two men do meet, here, by Bratley Water. Failing to recognise each other in the dim light, they fight, with tragic results.

> Like stags full spent, among the bent,
> They dropped awhile to rest:
> When the young man drove his flaying knife
> Deep in the old man's breast.
> The old man drove his gun stock down
> Upon the young man's head,
> And side by side by the water brown
> Those yeomen twain lay dead.

Our way winds a little uphill through very old, pollarded oaks and sweet chestnuts. When you meet a gravel path bear left to a wider gravel crosstrack running along the western edge of Bratley Inclosure. Turn right and follow the gravel track to go through a gate to the A31. Cross the road and go through the gate immediately opposite. Walk straight ahead to a gravel track. Bear right along this track, then right again to follow the track through a gate into Slufters Inclosure.

Slufters is mainly a pine wood with a sprinkling of oaks still clinging to the banks of one of the head waters of the Bratley stream which runs through a shallow valley among the trees on our right. Keep straight on along the gravel track over a crosstrack. When you come to a gate go through it, over the minor road ahead and through the gate opposite. The path soon curves left and climbs gently uphill. Go over a crosstrack and follow the gravel to the top of the hill where you come to a crossways in a more open area. Turn right and you will see a green way running downhill immediately on your right. Follow this path downhill through the oak trees and over the bridge which crosses the stream. The shallow valley is pretty here with the water flowing lazily around the roots of the oaks. And it is a favourite haunt of large green woodpeckers. We saw the bright colouring of several as we rested on the bridge.

Climb the slope opposite, folllowing the path through a grove of young pines to a gate. Beyond the gate you have a different scene — the wide expanse of Ocknell Plain. Go through the gate and take the path directly ahead over the plain. We are aiming for a little oak wood and you will see the rounded shape of the trees ahead. Walk over a crosstrack and follow an old wartime runway towards the wood. These runways are, of course, part of the wartime airfield at Stoney Cross. In 1944 the whole Forest area was used to conceal the troops and armaments massed for the Normandy landings.

Keep on past the wood until you meet another runway. Turn left and follow this long runway until you come to a Forestry Commission barrier. Look right now and you will see another barrier over a track into Ocknell Inclosure. Turn right to walk past the barrier and into the wood. Follow the track for a few yards then bear right along a wide way. This leads you through one of the most beautiful woods of unpollarded oaks and beeches in the Forest. Unlike the short, twisting, branching trunks of the trees in Bushy Bratley, these soar in great cathedral-like arches.

As we walked between the silver-grey trunks of the beeches we became aware of two large bright brown eyes watching us. There was no movement. A fallow doe lay resting among the matching fallen leaves only a few yards from our path. She did not move as we went past.

Cross the bridge over Highland Water and when the path divides keep straight on (right-hand path) to cross another small stream. Keep straight ahead to come out of Ocknell Inclosure onto the runways of Stoney Cross airfield, now a camping area.

The airfield was opened in November 1942. It became operational the following February with numbers 26, 175 and 239 Squadrons. In August 297 Squadron arrived with Albemarles and Whitleys. Later 299 Squadron was formed first with Venturas and then with Stirlings. Late in 1943 an American contingent came over and the following year 367 Fighter group arrived with P-38 Lightnings. In July they moved out to Normandy, and Stoney Cross was handed back to the RAF. Various operations took place including trooping flights to India before the station closed in October 1946.

Cross the runways and go over the heath to the minor road you will see directly ahead. Turn right and walk along this road for a short distance to where it crosses the A31 at Stoney Cross. The bus stop for Southampton is close by on your left. To return to your car, cross the main road and follow the Emery Down road straight ahead to the car park on the right.

Walk 24

ABOVE THE AVON VALLEY: A FOREST PANORAMA

Starting point: Bus: Forest Corner, off A31, about one mile east of Ringwood. Car: beside minor road to Hightown and Crow, off A31, near Forest Corner.

Distance: 4½ miles.

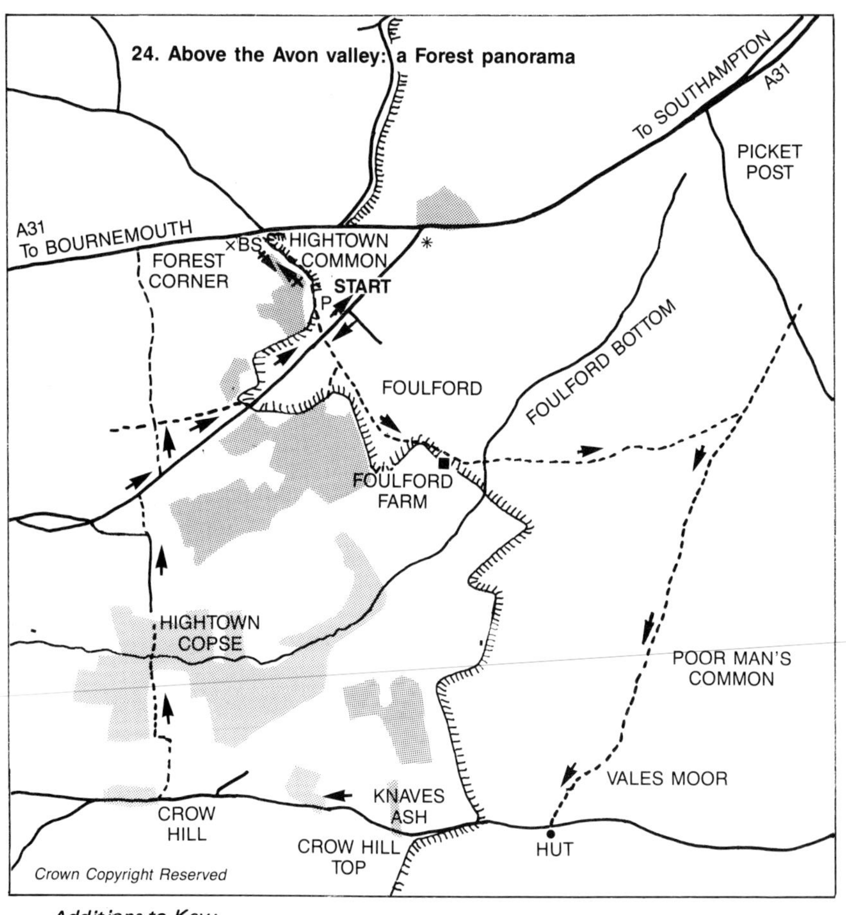

Additions to Key:
  × *Memorial*
  ✻ *Road to Hightown and Crow*   *For general Key see p. viii*

This walk is only about four and a half miles round, and you really will have the Forest at your feet! You follow an ancient greenway along one of the Forest's highest ridges of moorland and enjoy wonderful views as you walk. To the south, woods and heaths ripple towards the horizon formed by the curving blue line of the Isle of Wight hills. To the north-west, where the Forest trees edge the hillside above the Avon valley, you look over the green of the valley to the Wiltshire Downs.

If you come by bus, your starting point is Forest Corner, a stop beside the A31 on the hill above Ringwood, about a mile from Picket Post. Coming from Southampton, catch the Bournemouth bus which is routed through Ringwood. You have a pleasant if rather long journey across the Forest to its western boundary at Forest Corner. From the bus stop, turn right along a gravel track, over a cattle grid. Now turn left along a footpath leading over the heath. The path runs to the left of a hedge. Bear right along the path a short way to meet a minor road which runs to Ringwood through Hightown. Cross straight over the road and follow the path leading ahead to 'Foresters' and 'Foulford Farm'.

If you are arriving by car, this minor road is your starting point. Follow the A31 towards Ringwood. About a mile past Picket Post you will see the minor road on your left signposted Hightown and Crow. Turn left and follow this for a quarter of a mile — over a cattle grid — to an open area on the right where there is room to park. (This is just past a gravel road on your left.) Walk on down the road towards Hightown for a short distance and you will see the path to 'Foresters' and 'Foulford Farm' on your left.

Turn left and walk over the heath. The noise of traffic quickly fades and the peace of the Forest surrounds you. As I walked in a strong westerly wind, I experienced what is known in the Forest as 'clulberry weather', now a hint of rain, now a moment of dazzling sunshine, the cloud shadows dancing over the heath bringing constantly changing colours and contrasts.

The track divides in front of a white house. Keep straight on down the left hand of the two tracks. In front of you runs the high ridge followed by the greenway we are to take. Our path dips into a valley beside woods of old firs and beeches below the ridge. You now walk through an old oak wood, hidden in the valley, the spreading branches of the trees wreathed in blackthorn. Pass a Forest farm with a thatched barn on the right and keep straight on past a Forestry Commission barrier. You walk through more oak woods down to a stream. We cross this little stream again as it flows, copper-coloured, to meet the Avon, later in our walk.

Cross the bridge and climb the track up the heath ahead in the direction of the ridge. Several paths straggle up the first rise of this part of the hill. Keep on as straight ahead as you can and you will find that they merge into a well-marked track. Follow this main track — a white scar climbing the ridge — to the top.

As you climb the country unfolds with spreading views all around you. Behind is the valley with its sunny oak woods, and away to the west opens the Avon valley framed by soft waves of blue hills. I was enjoying the view when I saw to my surprise a herd of fallow deer within a few feet of me. I had walked right past them — they had not noticed me nor I them. I counted sixteen and so perfectly did their plain dun-coloured winter coats match the heathland that without their white rumps I believe I would not have seen them, close as they were. In Summer their coats are golden brown with white spots, in Winter they change to this darker shade that makes them almost invisible in woods as well as on heaths. Fallow deer in parks can have coats of either shade but do not change in this way.

As you reach flatter ground at the top of the ridge, you come to the wide greenway. This beautiful, banked route runs the whole length of the hillside over Poor Man's Common, where we are standing, to Picket Post a little to our left. It commands a marvellous view over all the surrounding countryside and is possibly a very old track indeed. Turn right and walk along this lovely path. To the left is the Forest with Burley Hill Fort rising dramatically from the heath and in front the Avon valley. A smaller hill on your left is Verely, a reminder of the Forest's smuggling days. This ridge way was a favourite smuggler's route from Highcliffe where goods were landed, across the Forest to Picket Post where there were underground cellars for storage. A woman called Lovey Warne took an active part in these proceedings. Wearing a conspicuous red cloak she would stand on Verely Hill to warn the smugglers if the Revenue men were about. I found it hard to believe that anyone could use so lofty a route to smuggle anything along but I believe I found the answer. A few yards to the left of the raised greenway, running parallel with it, is a deep sunken path, wide enough for men and pack animals. Choose an area where the gorse has been burnt to have a look along it. The path is deep enough to conceal people from even close observers. A similar smuggler's track crosses Ridley Wood, a mile east of Picket Post.

The path falls sharply to bring you off the ridge down to the minor road that runs through Burley Street towards Ringwood and Crow. Descend the ridge towards the road in the direction of a small hut behind a Forestry Commission barrier. Over the hillside to your left the sunken smuggler's track runs down beside a car park to continue over Cranes Moor. Turn right to walk on the heath beside the road past Knaves Ash House towards Crow Hill top. You pass a minor road on your keft.

We are now crossing the Forest boundary and this border area is full of interest. The large holes on the slopes beyond Knaves Ash, which were used as a rifle range, are said to have been dug originally as shelter by Cromwell's troops on their way through this hostile part of the country from Dorset to London. Crow Hill has been a settlement since the eleventh century and was once quite a busy place. A primitive form of brick-making took place here; the clay being dug from a pond in the Autumn and trodden with bare feet in the Spring when the bricks were made. They were baked in kilns heated by gorse from the Forest. Gloves were also made here and one of the present inhabitants remembers helping her mother to knit them. She was only five, just old enough to knit the straightforward plain and purl cuffs!

We follow the road for about three quarters of a mile in all. You come over Crow Hill top and pass a white bungalow on your right called 'Blue Haze'. Our way is down the next grass and gravel track on your right along the edge of a small copse that borders the road. Look carefully for this as the footpath sign that used to indicate this right of way is now missing. Turn right with the thickest part of the copse on your left. After a few yards you enter a splendid path bordered by tall oaks. When you come to a gate into a field, go through the gate, turn left along the edge of the field then right beside a wood down to a bridge. This takes you over the stream we crossed earlier in the oak wood. From the bridge follow the path bearing slightly right then straight uphill through Hightown Copse, a lovely oak and beech wood. I walked through a carpet of white wood anemones. Each delicate flower poised above its rosette of leaves moves with every breath of wind, so no wonder they are also called windflowers. You come out of the wood to follow a path beside some houses. Cross a stile, pass the houses on your right and keep straight on along the lane ahead.

When the lane curves left keep straight on along the footpath ahead through a wood. This brings you to a minor road. Turn right beside the road for just a few yards then turn left following the footpath sign. Follow the path to a crossing track. Turn right and follow this track past a mixture of modern houses and old Forest cottages to join the Hightown road again further south just before the Forest boundary.

Cross the cattle grid and walk beside the road over the heath until you come to the point where we originally turned down the path to 'Foulford Farm' and 'Foresters'. To return to the bus stop turn left and retrace the route to the hedge round the white house. Follow the path back to the cattle grid beside the A31 at Forest Corner. To catch a return bus to Southampton, cross the road to the stop in front of a Nursery.

To return to your car just continue the short distance up the road towards the A31. But before doing so you might like to follow the track, left, to the bus stop at Forest Corner where there is a memorial to a remarkable man. A carved stone commemorates Baron Eversley, a pioneer in the preservation of areas of outstanding beauty. He fought a thirty-year campaign through the law courts of England to resist the enclosure of common lands during the latter half of the nineteenth century. In 1864 he launched the Commons Preservation Society which succeeded in establishing a principle in law recognising the right of all to enjoy the countryside with access to famous viewpoints. He fought for the preservation of footpaths and public rights of way and in 1894 published an account of this work under the title *Commons, Forests and Footpaths*. It is right that so fine a man should be remembered here on this lofty hillside.

• THE SOUTHERN FOREST •

Although this area verges on the spreading belt of coastal towns and villages it still holds magnificent woodlands and remote valleys which are as interesting in their own way as any in the less accessible north. Sir Walter Scott was reminded of his native Scotland by these southern moors, particularly around Holmsley where we walk. Just over what is now the southern boundary of the Forest, in the small village of Boldre, Robert Southey — once Poet Laureate — lived with his second wife, Catherine Bowles. Both were inspired by the Forest scenery. Early in the eighteenth century, when wild country was considered barbarous and ugly, William Gilpin, vicar of Boldre, fostered the new appreciation of its beauty by his descriptions of his surroundings. It was in the south too that Captain Marryat set *The Children of the New Forest*.

Many of the Forest's most fascinating wetlands are to be found in the south which provide a wealth of interesting plants. Forest bogs, easily identifiable by the white plumes of cotton grass, are best avoided but growing in the damp valleys you will find the aromatic bog myrtle, yellow bog asphodel and insect-trapping sundews and, if you are lucky, the rare marsh gentian and royal fern.

Walk 25

HOLMSLEY AND THORNEY HILL

Starting point: Osmonds Bushes car park (near Holmsley Station — disused). Bus: Holmsley Station.

Distance: About eight miles.

Campsite: Holmsley.

Holmsley is one of the most intriguing of the Forest Inclosures. It is a strange wood of ancient trees, whose roots rise out of a wide marsh, which is brilliant with wild flowers. This walk takes us through Holmsley which lies south of Burley and across the heath to Thorney Hill on the south-western boundary of the Forest. It is a wonderful walk if you like the open heathlands of the Forest with splendid views towards Burley from Holmsley Ridge.

If you are camping at Holmsley campsite you are perfectly placed for this walk

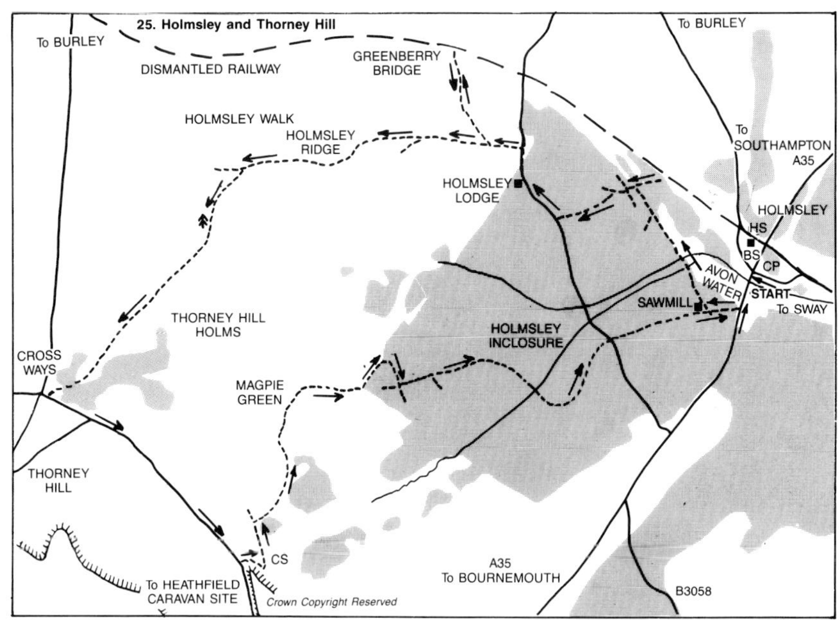

Additions to Key:
HS Holmsley Station (dis.) Now tearooms   *CP Osmund's Bushes car park*
CS Holmsley campsite
Pine tree. (Route marker)   *For general Key see p. viii*

as the route passes the site. I will indicate your joining point in the text.

Our starting point, if you come by car, is Osmonds Bushes car park, close to the now disused Holmsley Station. Travelling from Southampton take the A35 west in the direction of Bournemouth. Immediately after crossing the bridge at Holmsley turn left down a minor road signposted to Burley and Sway. Just past the corner turn left again into Osmonds Bushes car park. It is concealed as you come round the corner so you need to signal early and turn immediately. From the car park entrance, turn right to the A35. Turn left and walk beside the road for about fifty yards before you turn right through a gate opening onto a gravel track leading to a sawmill.

Arriving by bus, alight at Holmsley Station. Turn right along the A35 (direction of Bournemouth) and turn right through the gate to the sawmill.

Follow the track to a gate but do not go through it. Turn right just in front of it and go past a Forestry Commission barrier and along the path ahead which soon becomes a wide raised way leading through the mysterious wood I mentioned which looks more like a miniature version of the Florida everglades than a New Forest wood.

Dwarf oak trees twined with ivy and protected by thorn bushes rise from the marshes on either side and occasionally small bridges lead you over a network of shallow streams among thickets of irises and marsh marigolds. Beyond the oaks stand islands of silver birches, equally distorted and overgrown, their bright bark and wine-coloured shoots contrasting with the more sombre, blue-green of the lichens shrouding the oaks. Everywhere, floating in great carpets, we saw the white flowers of the frogbit above their round flat leaves. It is a fascinating place.

Walk past the first gate on the left into the Inclosure and keep straight ahead to the next gate by a crosstrack. Turn left through this gate. After a few yards four paths converge on our route. Turn right and take the left hand of the two paths you see ahead of you. This climbs uphill with a plantation of young pines on your left and a mixture of oaks and more mature pines on your right. Follow this green path as it brings you to a spacious grove of larger oak trees beside a gate leading onto a minor road. Turn right and walk along the road for about a hundred yards. You pass Holmsley Lodge on your left and cross a cattle grid. A few yards over the grid turn left along a gravel track leading over the open heath above Holmsley Ridge. At the edge of the heath, against a backdrop of dark trees, you pass a Forest homestead. Walk for only a few yards along the gravel path until you see a narrow path leading past a barrier off our way on the right. Turn right to follow this path through the high gorse, to see one of the loveliest views in the New Forest; the view that reminded Walter Scott of his beloved Border country. The ground dips away and before you unfolds the wide Holmsley valley with the narrow Avon river running through it. Beyond the river, the heathlands climb to a long line of Forest trees which fringe the whole length of the horizon.

Follow the path downhill to Greenberry Bridge which arches the track of the railway that formerly crossed the Forest between Brockenhurst and Ringwood. Now the line is a green way, its steep embankments scoring the length of the valley with a definite beauty of its own. You will see the white chimney of a former gate keeper's cottage just showing over a fold in the heath.

Retrace your steps to the gravel track beyond the homestead. Turn right past another barrier and walk west over the heath towards Thorney Hill. To the left stands the dark mass of Holmsley Inclosure but here you are truly on the high Forest heath with the air full of the song of skylarks. Although there are so many larks, they can be difficult to see. However, there is some rather noticeable white in their tail feathers and a small crest on their heads which they raise when they are disturbed or excited. They have an endearing way of walking, not hopping!

When the gravel track turns left to a gravel pit keep straight on along the heathland path. After about a mile the track divides. Follow the left hand of the tracks as it leads a little downhill. Our path is now obscured in places and for the next hundred yards or so you need to navigate carefully. Ahead of you you will see one lonely Scots pine (not the one over to your left). Pick your way towards it keeping a patch of tall gorse bushes on your left. When you reach the pine you will find a very narrow track running straight ahead with the pine a little to your right.

Beyond the pine the heath drops to a shallow valley. Its treacherous marshy nature is revealed by the white tufts of cotton grass which cover it like a fluffy blanket. Heather is also a good guide. The deep pink calluna, or ling, which blossoms early will only grow on dry ground. But tread carefully where you find a small heather with pink flowers arranged in groups of four down its stem — the *Erica tetralix* or cross-leaved heather. It thrives in damp, boggy places.

Follow the narrow path as it winds its way to another part of the Forest which has a rather mysterious atmosphere, Thorney Hill Holms. Three dark yew trees greet you at the approach to this strange wood mainly composed of yews and enormous, tangled hollies, or holms. The heavy shade is broken only rarely to allow small glades of ferns. I was not surprised to be told that our path through the holms is called the Devil's Walk. This wood was once a favourite haunt of the gypsies and not so long ago we would have seen the smoke from their camp fires, heard the Romany speech and possibly had our fortunes told.

When you come to a small green lawn cross over and follow the track straight ahead between the hollies. This brings you to a barrier before a minor road running between Thorney Hill village and Hinton called Forest Road. (A few yards to your right is Crossways where our road meets another road from Thorney Hill to Bransgore.)

Turn left along Forest Road. Thorney Hill village is on the right and open heathland on the left. We are now following the smuggler's road which ran inland from favourite coastal landings like Chewton Bunny through Hinton — where stands the Cat and Fiddle Inn once a refuge for smugglers — through Thorney Hill to Burley. The Forest provided ideal cover until well inland.

Follow the road until it turns right for Heathfield Caravan Site and you see a large sign for Holmsley Campsite on your left. (This is your starting point if you are camping here.) Turn left at the sign, then follow the old tracks of the disused airfield first left again to skirt the campsite and leave a small wood on your right. Just past the wood you will see another track leading right past a barrier. Turn right and follow this as it leads over the heath towards Magpie Green.

The concrete path we are following is a reminder of the part the Forest played in the last world war. Apart from the airfields, the Forest was a training ground for troops. Vehicles for the D-Day landings were pushed along these tracks to be hidden among the trees. The whole Forest was alive with troops and equipment preparing for the landings yet all these preparations remained a secret!

The track bears a little left then firmly right to bring you to the western corner of Holmsley Inclosure. Turn left before the Inclosure and walk for a short distance until you see a stile leading into the Inclosure on your right. Go over the stile to a crosstrack. Turn left here and when the path divides keep straight on (left-hand path) and follow the track as it dips downhill over an attractive stream, a tributary of the Avon. This tiny thread of water bustles busily along beneath a canopy of overhanging tree-roots with, here and there, paths worn over its sides by the deer seeking drinking places.

Our way turns to bear left, uphill, to bring us to a gate opening onto a minor road. Cross the road and go through the gate immediately opposite. This path leads to the other side of the sawmill. Walk over the sawmill yard and through the gate. You are now back on the track you followed earlier to turn right into that strange world of marsh and oak woods. (If you started the walk at Holmsley campsite turn left and follow the path past the Forestry Commission barrier into Holmsley Inclosure to continue the route as directed.)

Retrace your steps to the A35 and turn left for Osmonds Bushes. A pleasant end to this walk is to cross to Holmsley Station where the former station buildings are now tearooms. The bus stop is close by.

Walk 26

EXPLORING BOLDRE VILLAGE

Starting point: Car and bus: Setley New Inn, off A337, near Brockenhurst.

Distance: 6½ miles.

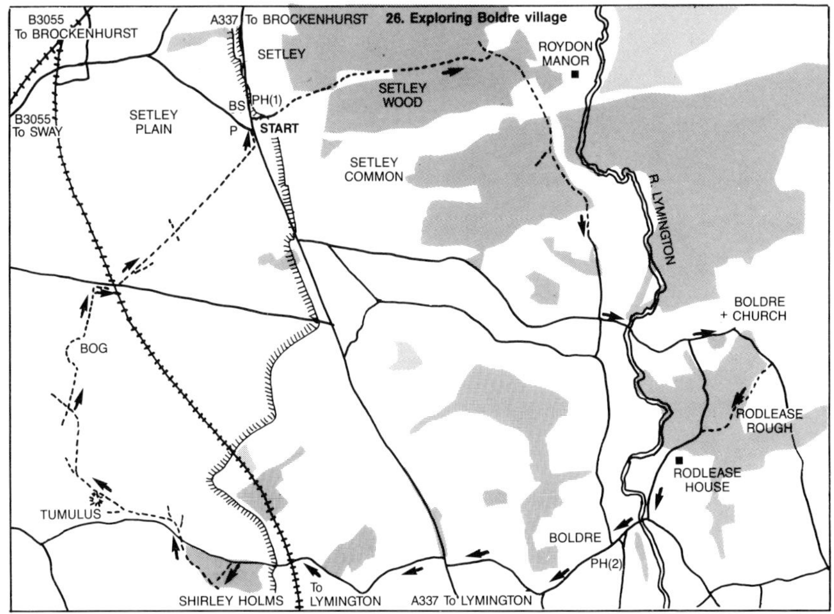

Additions to Key:
PH(1) *Filly Inn*   BS *Setley New Inn bus stop*
PH(2) *Red Lion Inn*   P   *Parking*   *For general Key see p. viii*

It is easy to miss Boldre, a quiet, rather remote village, tucked away in the Forest beside the river a mile or two north of Lymington. But it is a fascinating place with a wealth of stories to add to our Forest lore. You will find an ancient church where Robert Southey, better known as a Lake District writer, married his second wife, New Forest poetess Catherine Bowles. We pass a house used by smugglers, a school built by a local man in gratitude when the villagers rescued him from pirates, and find out why a special service is held every year in the church which draws people from many different parts of the British Isles. A great many of the houses around Boldre and in the village itself were built during the eighteenth century, restful and satisfying in their design. So you will find Boldre lovely to look at as well as interesting.

Our walk starts from close to the Filly Inn at Setley, a mile south of Brockenhurst on the A337 to Lymington. Driving from Brockenhurst, follow the Lymington road until you come to the Filly Inn on the left. Just past the Inn, you will see a minor road signposted to New Milton and Sway on your right. Turn into this road and you will find space to park beyond the bus stop. For those using public transport the bus service is number 56 running from Southampton via Brockenhurst to Lymington. Our route begins from the stop on the corner of the Sway road known as 'Setley New Inn'. The stop to catch the bus back to Brockenhurst is opposite. The walk is about six and a half miles round.

From the bus stop at the corner of the Sway road, cross the A337 to a narrow lane marked with a No Through Road sign. Follow the lane as it dips downhill into Setley Wood. Go through the gate into the wood following the public bridle-way. I was startled as I walked along the dry path by a large, coal-black rabbit which appeared suddenly under the gorse bushes, looked at me for a moment then scampered off to join his more ordinary companions who took no notice of me at all! Our way runs through groves of silver birches and stands of enormous Scots pines. The pines, their flaking russet bark overlaid in patterns like wave marks on a beach, are some of the most beautiful I have seen. Among them stands the occasional solitary twisted shape of an ancient oak, a survivor of former woods.

When a path joins our way from the left keep on along the main track, bearing a little right, past the lodge at the gates of Roydon Manor and keep straight on following the direction indicated by the footpath sign. The lane here is bordered by more ancient oaks, their branches contorted and embossed to such an extent that it is easy to imagine goblin faces among them and to understand why the Forest is so full of tales of Puck and his fellow hobgoblins, taking a mischievous delight in leading travellers astray. We find a wood called 'Puckpits', 'Puckmoor' and a burial mound, or barrow, on Beaulieu common which was once known as 'Pixey's cave'. I saw no goblins, only the inquisitive face of a squirrel glancing down at me with his shiny shoe-button eyes!

Our pleasant lane leads to a crossroads. Turn left for Boldre church. Before reaching the church you cross a bridge over the Boldre, or Lymington river. Here the river flows strongly through lush meadows dotted with dreamy-looking cattle. Willows trail in the water and below the bridge is a small island, golden with kingcups in the Spring and edged by long weed fronds waving snakily under the surface. Ducks quack busily about in the shallows to complete a perfect picture!

From the stream climb the lane to Boldre Church which overlooks the valley. The church of St John the Baptist at Boldre dates from the twelfth century, though there may well have been an earlier church on the site. Its distance from the village is probably due to its original purpose, to serve as a 'halfway house' for the monks travelling to Christchurch and Beaulieu. Traditionally, Boldre church door key was removed from Beaulieu Abbey at its dissolution in 1539.

Inside, the church welcomes you with its homely weathered stone and comfortable-looking box pews. Allow some time to look round as it is full of interest. And now you will find strange faces looking down at you! These are the carved bosses in the roof of the nave, some of them very devilish in expression. There are traces of medieval wall paintings and in a glass case is a rare 'breeches' Bible — so called because in this edition it was considered more decorous for Adam and Eve to make themselves breeches out of fig leaves than the usual aprons. And here, in his own church, hangs a portrait of Boldre's most famous vicar, William Gilpin. He was presented with the living in 1777 at a time when, it was said, his parishioners were notorious as little better than a set of bandits! Apart from writing his book on the 'picturesque' which made him famous, Gilpin worked hard for his parishioners, endowing a school and a house for the poor. In 1791 there is a fascinating entry in the church register. Two weddings were to be solemnised about the same time. When the customary registration tax of threepence was demanded, one of the bridegrooms objected; the other gallantly said he would pay for both of them, explaining that his wife would not be worth having if not considered worth an additional threepence. There is no record of what either wife paid! Apart from Gilpin, Boldre church has more literary associations. Here, poet laureate Robert Southey married his second wife, Catherine Bowles.

And now the twentieth century comes into our story. Boldre is known nationally as 'The Hood' church. HMS Hood, sunk in action against the Bismark in 1941, was the flagship of Vice-Admiral L E Holland who lost his life in the tragedy. He had been a regular worshipper at Boldre and his widow arranged for the memorial to be placed in the church. This includes an illuminated book of remembrance containing the names of all those who lost their lives; and a painting of HMS Hood given by the eminent marine artist, Montague Dawson. A commemoration service, attended by many relatives of the men who died in her, is held each year on a Sunday near to May 24, the date of her sinking.

From the church gate where you entered, turn left along the lane for a few yards then follow the lane as it turns right downhill to cross a stream. A few yards up the hill brings you to a footpath sign on the right. Follow this path through a wood fringed by a hazel coppice. As I came this way in early Spring each hazel bud was breaking into twin leaves which hung along the boughs still a little crumpled, resembling tiny green socks pegged out to dry!

The path brings you down to a lane where you turn left for Boldre past Rodlease House. Smugglers used to 'borrow' the horses out of the stables at Rodlease at night and return them in the morning with their fee — a cask or two or good French brandy. Turn right at the next road junction to cross a fine five-arched stone bridge into Boldre.

As you walk up the hill through the village, past elegant eighteenth century houses, look for Boldre Lane, a small road on the left. When I first came this way, I found an attractive old house on the left which was the village shop and post office. Then, the village shopkeeper told me that the neighbouring house with windows set in wide pointed arches was originally a school with a small house for the teacher attached to it. The story connected with it was a fascinating one. Evidently the owner of Tweed House (we shall be passing this large house shortly) was unlucky enough to be captured by pirates. The pirates demanded a ransom which the villagers paid, and in gratitude he built a school for their children when he returned. On my last visit I found that the school is now a private house lovingly restored by the owners who found a plaque recording this event in their garden. The plaque is now in the porch and reads: 'In thankful Memory of Deliverance from Brigands of the province of Salerno in Italy by payment of a Ransom of L5100 after 102 days captivity in the year 1865 W J C Moens of Tweed Esquire erected this Church of England School AD 1869.' The story was told to me as if it all happened yesterday and somehow you feel very close to the past in Boldre.

Memories of the Civil War linger long in the Forest. Until recently, in Boldre, on Oakapple Day the children wore sprigs of oak. Non-wearers were greeted with cries of 'sheet shacks', an old word for an oakapple.

Pass the half-timbered Red Lion Inn and climb Rope Hill. Tweed House is on the left of the road. The name 'Rope Hill' is a reminder of the days when rope making was a Forest industry. At the top of the hill we meet the A337 again. Turn right beside the road for only a few yards, then left down the minor road signposted Shirley Holms; another intriguing name and as fascinating a place as the name suggests! Follow the road under the railway and you come to the Holms. 'Holms' are hollies and here is the most extraordinary oak wood — each tall tree is ringed by its attendant hollies which have grown long sinuous trunks as if they wished to imitate the oaks. So the hollies spread dark branches overhead, just beneath the level of the oak tree boughs.

After the railway bridge follow the path that runs parallel with the minor road through the Holms and you walk beneath an evergreen canopy of sparkling holly leaves twisted as they are to point all ways to catch the light. You pass Shirley Holms Manor on your right and to see more of these immense hollies, turn left when you come to a Forestry Commission barrier — just before you come to the New Forest Equestrian Centre on your right. This path leads you through the Holms to emerge on an open hillside. Turn right here on a crossing track and follow this main track as it curves to bring you back to the Shirley Holms road again beside a car park.

We have about a mile and a half of heathland to cross on our right to return to our starting point at Setley. Cross the road and immediately in front of you is a Forestry Commission barrier with several tracks radiating from it. Take the path furthest left which runs to the right of the road, almost parallel with it at first. When the path divides keep to the left hand track. Ahead you will see a large, gorse-covered mound — a Bronze Age burial mound or tumulus. The path now divides again. Bear right towards the tumulus. When you are close to the tumulus follow the track as it bears right to bring you to a fork. Turn right at the fork. Shortly you come to a crosstrack. Turn right and follow the path for a few yards. You will see the line of the path we are following leading straight ahead to a minor road with a railway bridge a little to the right. Unfortunately our path — once a raised green way — has now become very boggy directly ahead so bear left along the joining path you will see before the boggy area. This curves right to bring you back to our original path after the worst of the marsh. Follow the path straight ahead to the minor road.

Turn right along the minor road, under the railway, and immediately on your left you will see a good track leading you over Setley Plain. Follow this uphill over all crosstracks and soon you will see the white walls, black shutters and tall chimneys of the Filly Inn about half a mile distant. Keep straight ahead following a slightly raised path in the direction of the A337 and the Inn. The green path brings you back to the A337 a few yards from our destination. Turn left at the fence before the road to return to your car or the bus stop at the corner of the Sway and New Milton road.

This walk is really a journey into time. I am sure you will enjoy it as much as I did!

Walk 27

SWAY, SET THORNS AND HINCHESLEA:
Some Forest Mysteries

Starting point: Bus, car, train: Sway Station.

Distance: 5½ miles.

Campsite: Setthorns (open all the year).

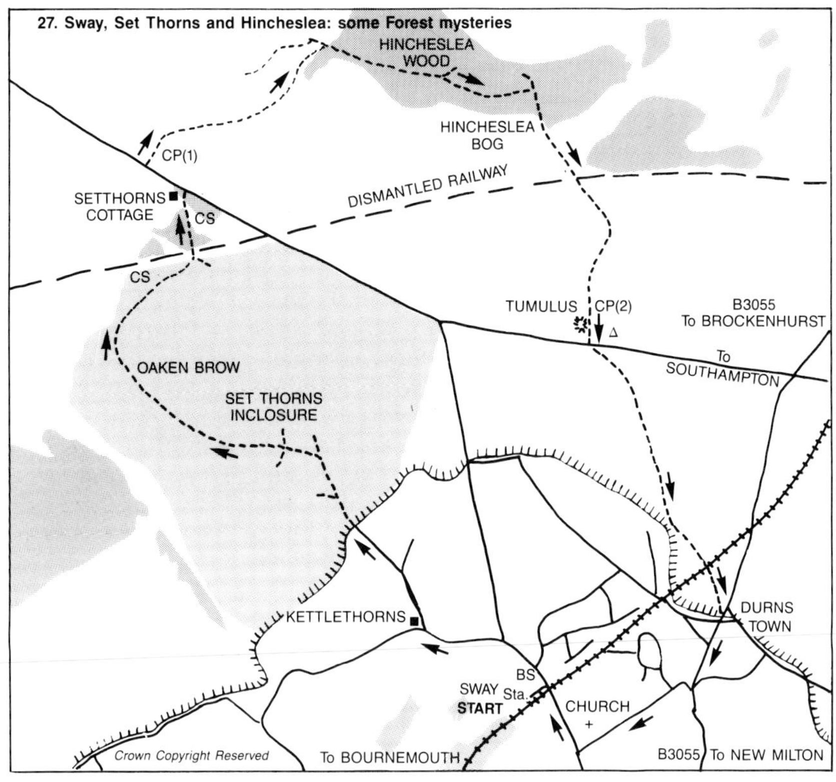

Additions to Key:

Sta *Sway Station*	△ *Triangulation point*
CS *Setthorns campsite*	*For general Key see p. viii*
CP(1) *Horseshoe Bottom car park*	
CP(2) *Longslade View car park*	

At first glance there seems to be nothing mysterious about Sway but follow this walk to discover differently! Sway appears to be a quiet village to the south of the Forest in the area where Captain Marryat set his *Children of the New Forest*, a few miles north of Lymington. It lies each side of the Southampton to Bournemouth railway and is now just outside the official southern boundary of the Forest. It is, however, still a true Forest village and, as you will find out, a place of fascinating mysteries.

The first puzzle I had to solve concerned Sway's exact position. Old maps show the village close to the little hamlet of Tiptoe so in the last hundred years Sway has moved a mile and a half west! The answer lies in the coming of a new railway. I discovered that Tiptoe was the original area of Sway, a much smaller place than today's village. During Victorian days the boom in seaside development turned the sleepy hamlet of Bourne into the flourishing resort of Bournemouth. People wanted seaside holidays and the existing railway, laid in the mid-nineteenth century, was of little use to them. It ran from Southampton to a point about a mile south of Brockenhurst, then west across the Forest through Wimborne Minster to Poole. So a new line was laid from just south of Brockenhurst to take them to Bournemouth. At the same time inclosures were made in the Sway area. So Sway moved to its present position as a home both for the railway workers and the folk engaged in forestry. The result of this mixture of old and new gives Sway a special attraction; you will find that ancient cob-walled cottages blend happily here with Victorian brick.

Our walk, about five and a half miles round, starts from Sway Station. (I will indicate in the text your joining point if you are camping at Setthorns.) Buses from Lymington and Lyndhurst stop here. If you are driving, take the A337 (Lymington road) from Lyndhurst to Brockenhurst. Just before the village, turn right following the signs for Sway. Go straight over the next cross roads again following the Sway signs. As you come into Sway village follow the signs for the Station. There are several parking areas nearby and a Station car park down the first lane on your left as you approach the railway bridge with the shopping area on your right.

It is pleasant to make the journey by train on the Southampton–Bournemouth line. As you come out of the station notice the date carved over the entrance — 1886 — too late for the original railway but right of course for the later one laid to Bournemouth. Walk up the lane from the Station to the bridge in Station Road then turn left to walk up the road through the village. (If you have parked in Station Road, you will have the Station on your left.) You come to a fork. Our way is left here, down Mead End road. The other lane is called Brighton road, named after one of the gangs who came here to lay the railway. Another gang came from Manchester and gave their name to a road we pass on our return route. Walk a short way down Mead End road, then turn right down Adlams Lane which leads to Set Thorns Inclosure. On the corner you pass a house with the enchanting name of Kettlethorns.

It Happened in Hampshire tells us that a secret passage used by smugglers connects Kettlethorns with the sea. Another passage, four miles long, connected Sway House with the coast. South of Sway, leading off Silver Street, is Agars Lane, so frequently used by smugglers that it is said that the deep ruts formed by their waggon wheels may still be traced! Presumably the smugglers would lead their ponies down Adlams Lane to cross the Forest.

It is a lovely lane, bordered by oaks, and dipping down to a footpath. Soon you come to a gate opposite Set Thorns Inclosure. Go through the gate, cross the green lawn ahead, and through another gate into the wood. We had just closed the gate when a troupe of fallow deer with their distinctive white rumps ran across our path, heads held high, causing the faintest of rustling among the dead bracken as they disappeared among the oak trees. Our way heads west through Set Thorns

Inclosure then curves right to bring us out of the wood and over the old railway track at Setthorns cottage. Ignore the first left turn but when the path divides, bear left here. Traditional oaks and holly border the left side of our track, the other side is fringed by tall larches inter-planted with young pines. Now keep to this main track, straight over all crossways. Set Thorns is a maze of paths rambling up and down hill. If you cannot resist some of these tempting ways, you could ramble round the Inclosure and return to Sway by one of several routes which a glance at the map would suggest.

William Gilpin rode through Set Thorns at the end of the eighteenth century. (His parish at Boldre included Sway.) He comments sadly that once Set Thorns 'was the noblest of all Forest scenes, the number of its oaks were the admiration of all who saw them. But its glories are now over. During the unremitted course of thirty years it continued to add strength to the fleets of Britain; itself sufficient to raise a Navy. In this arduous service its vigour was at length exhausted; and it contains little more at present than shrubs and underweed . . .'. Today we are more fortunate. The mighty oaks may have gone, but with the careful replanting of Set Thorns we can enjoy some of its former glory.

Our way curves round to the right round Oaken Brow to lead through part of the wood where you can see a plantation of young, healthy pines on your left. This planting and harvesting of quick-growing timber is vital if the Forest is to 'pay its way' in the twentieth century. But the Forestry Commission also ensures that the beauty of the Forest is maintained and safeguarded. The work of the Commission who administer the Forest is extremely varied. Under their care, the Forest is replanted so that the old woods — the 'ancient and ornamental woodlands' — are preserved and at the same time softwoods are planted and harvested to make sure the Forest is economically viable as well as beautiful. The Commission works closely with the New Forest Consultation Panel who represent all who have interests in the Forest. They include the Commoners who need land cleared and drained for their animals. Conservationists, residents, campers, and walkers are also represented.

Soon you will see Setthorns Campsite ahead. (If you are staying here it is the ideal place from which to begin this circular walk. It is a beautiful site with woodland pitches and open throughout the year.) Go through the barrier and follow the gravel track ahead through the pines with the campsite on your left. When you come to a T-junction turn left to cross the bridge over the disused railway. Follow the path uphill to the site entrance. Turn right and walk the few yards to a minor road. Turn left (Setthorns Cottage is on your left) and follow the road to a car park — Horseshoe Bottom — on your right. Go right along the gravel track leading into the car park keeping straight ahead to a barrier. Now you overlook a beautiful green expanse of turf, cropped short by the Forest ponies, called Long Slade Bottom.

This is how Gilpin describes our view, nearly two hundred years ago. You will find it has changed very little! 'A beautiful valley, about a quarter of a mile in breadth, opened before us, arrayed in vivid green, and winding two or three miles round a wood. On the other side the grounds, wild and unadorned, fall with an easy sweep into it. Beyond these a grand woody scene spreads far and wide into the distance . . . the valley was no other than that vast bog, Longslade Bottom. The nimble deer trips over it in summer without inconvenience, but no animals of heavier bulk dare trust themselves upon it . . .' But there is no need to worry about crossing it today. One change that has occurred is an improvement in drainage! A 'slade' in the Forest means a little valley between wooded hills, which is just what you see.

We intend making for the left hand corner of the wood you see on the other side of Long Slade: Hincheslea Wood. Over the green you will see our track clearly winding up the hillside towards the corner of the wood, the right hand of two paths. Cross the green to pick up the path and follow it uphill, north-east, through the heather and gorse, leaving a small wood on your right. Keep straight on along the main path to a clearing and a crosstrack. Turn right and follow this good worn way east along the brow of the hill with Hincheslea Wood on your left.

Half-hidden among the pines and undergrowth you will see remnants of ancient oaks, some only shells, survivors of the woods Gilpin regretted. Oak trees have always been specially vulnerable. Apart from their value as naval timber, their bark was used in tanning leather, a process known as 'rhining'. Sway was the centre of this Forest industry. The rhine was dried until it was brittle and a piece of rhine 'as big as a penny was worth a penny'.

Walk along the edge of Hincheslea Wood until the track divides. Keep straight on here (right-hand path) as our way runs a little downhill through the trees. Soon you come to a well-marked gravelled crosstrack. Turn right and follow the track as it plunges steeply downhill. This runs to the old railway again. Follow the path down and now we see some of the Forest's real wetlands. Our path is raised to cross shallow brooks widening into ponds full of tall waving sedge grasses. At one point an island of rhododendron bushes appears crowned by minute pine trees. As I walked past I heard the harsh croak of a heron from deep within the reeds. Follow the track ahead between the brick sides of a former railway bridge and up the heath opposite to a minor road at Long Slade View car park.

Before the road you pass another Bronze Age tumulus on the right of the path. Its soft green turf and sheltering gorse bushes make it an ideal place for a rest. From the tumulus look across the road and over the heath beyond to see a tall slim tower on the horizon beyond Sway.

It is known as Sway Tower or Peterson's Folly and may well qualify as another of Sway's puzzles! It was built between 1879 and 1884 by Andrew Thomas Turton Peterson, formerly a Judge of the High Court of Calcutta. One of the first buildings ever to be constructed of concrete, it was built without steel reinforcement by unskilled labour, 220 feet high with twelve rooms sixteen feet square one over the other, reached by a spiral staircase at the side. The Forest saying goes that there are as many steps in the tower as there are days in the year and as many windows as there are weeks! Mr Peterson wanted to put a light at the top, but was forbidden by the Board of Trade who suspected it would confuse shipping. But what could have led the retired judge to build such a home? Various stories circulate — one is that His Honour intended to be buried at the top and his wife at the bottom, thus, showing his superiority! If this were true, he was disappointed; Mrs Peterson was buried in Sway churchyard and Mr Peterson's ashes at the foot of his tower. In 1957 they were transferred to his wife's grave. Another story claims that Mr Peterson, being an ardent Spiritualist, received communications through a medium from Sir Christopher Wren. The great architect gave his pupil directions for mixing the concrete and pointed out to him errors in laying his foundations.

We are going to use this outstanding landmark to help us get our bearings right on the way back. Keeping your eyes on the tower, leaving the tumulus on your right, cross the minor road. The route now runs across the heath ahead in the direction of the tower. Follow the track you will see bearing a little left then curving towards the tower, ignoring all side tracks. Sway village becomes more noticeable on the hillside to your right. The long gentle curving line of the Isle of Wight downs forms the horizon ahead of us.

Cross the railway bridge and walk over the common to a cattle grid over the B3055. Turn right along this road through Durns Town. This is the oldest part of Sway and you will see several traditional Forest cottages. Durns Town may have derived its name from the family called Durrant who farmed here in the seventeenth and eighteenth centuries. Before that, in the Forest perambulation of 1670, it was called the hamlet of Stamford after the brook that now flows under the road at the foot of Back Lane. You will see Back Lane on the left, just before you come to a crossroads.

At the crossroads turn right up Church Lane. As you might expect, you pass Sway church, a pleasant early Victorian church built in the Gothic style. The church was built in 1938 when life in Sway had much more in common with the England of the first Queen Elizabeth! Bishop Sumner, arriving to consecrate the church a year later, came on horseback. Some ladies who were decorating the church told me, among many other stories about Sway which I have included in this chapter, that before the railway, horse-drawn cabs were driven through the Forest to Brockenhurst to collect visitors from London. You can hire horse-drawn wagons today in Burley (see p.   ) and Brockenhurst (see p.   ) so you can recapture some of the atmosphere of the Forest in the early nineteenth century.

Inside the church, I found more of Sway's mysteries. The church is dedicated to St Luke but on the foundation stone we read 'dedicated to St Mark'. What can we make of that? On the window sill in the north wall of the Sanctuary is an urn containing the ashes of an Egyptian christian who lived two hundred years after Christ. How did this find its way to St Luke's? On the north wall is an ancient crucifix found near Sway some years ago. How old? Who found it and where? Nobody appears to have the definite answers.

At the end of Church Lane turn right and you will see the Station ahead.

Walk 28

BY THE DARK WATER

Starting point: Car: Blackwell Common car park. Bus: Blackfield
Crossroads.

Distance: 5 miles.

In the south of the Forest the Beaulieu river tends to steal the limelight, but east of the Beaulieu there is a stream just as lovely in its much quieter way, the Dark Water. This walk of about five miles follows the valley of the Dark Water. If you like history — or crossing remote heathland — you might like to add a mile to this walk as an optional extra. I will describe this diversion later in our ramble.

Our starting point if you come by bus is the crossroads at Blackfield. From Southampton, catch one of the buses that run through Dibden and Hythe to Calshot. After going through Hardley, the bus leaves the A326 to turn for Lepe.

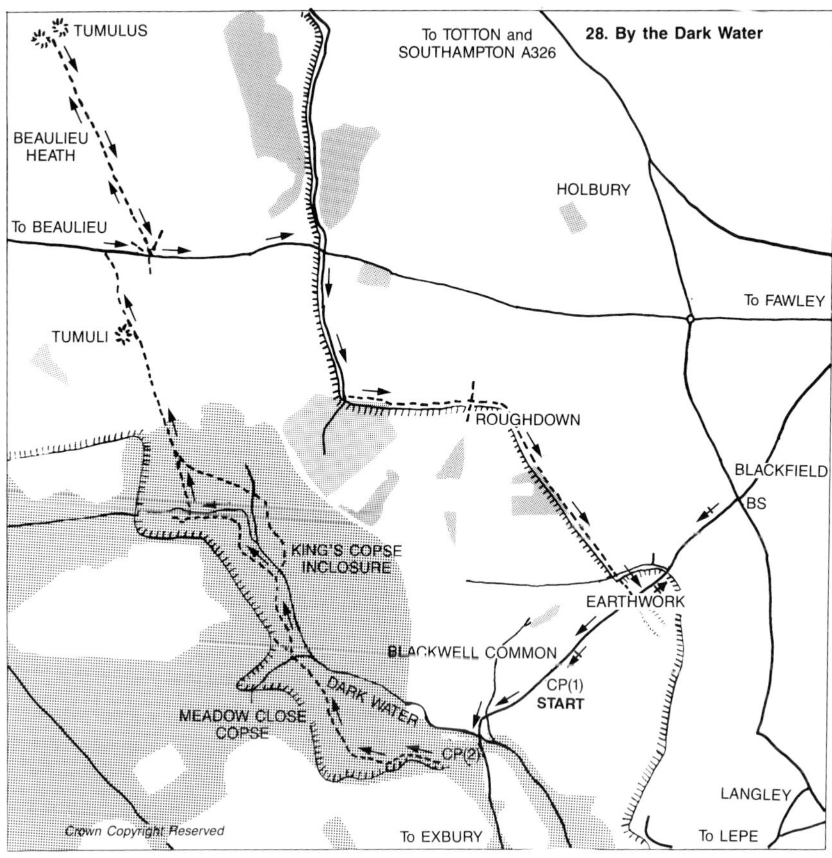

Additions to Key:

CP(1) *Blackwell Common car park*
CP(2) *Dark Water car park*

For general Key see p. viii

Blackfield crossroads is about a mile down this road. Alight at the Hampshire Yeoman Inn and walk the few yards back from the inn to the crossroads. Our way is left, down the road signposted to Exbury. Turn left and walk a short distance to a gate opening on to the quiet, heath-covered expanse of Blackwell Common. Immediately the peace of the Forest surrounds you as you leave all traces of the workaday world behind. Go through the gate and follow the road straight ahead towards a darkly-pencilled line of trees edging the common over the heath. You pass Blackwell car park on your left.

If you come by car, you can park on the Common at Blackwell car park. Take the A326 (Fawley road). Keep straight on through Hardley and turn right along the road signposted Blackfield and Lepe. You pass the Hampshire Yeoman Inn on your right and immediately turn right down the minor road signposted Exbury. Go over the cattle grid onto the heath and after a short distance you will come to a car park on your left — Blackwell Common. From the car park turn left to follow the road as it crosses the Common.

As you come closer to the trees ahead, King's Copse Inclosure, the road dips into the valley of the Dark Water. The stream forms the boundary of the heath; on the opposite hillside the trees crowd close to the water's edge. Cross the bridge and climb the road ahead through the woods. After about fifty yards you will see Dark Water car park on your right. You leave the road here to follow a foot-path. Turn right and walk across the gravel of the car park for a few yards towards a barrier. Turn left through the trees for a few yards to a good footpath running between the Inclosure fence and the gravel of the car park. Turn right and follow the path, keeping the Inclosure fence close on your left.

The way is wide and embanked and runs straight through the trees along the hillside west of the Dark Water. At this point the stream below in the valley is invisible under its screen of willows and oaks. Follow this path through glorious woods of oaks, hollies and beeches.

It was Spring when I came this way. The brown cones of the beech buds were uncurling to release still-crumpled leaves and the ground each side of the path was deep purple with violets.

The path leads deeper into King's Copse and the woodlands become more remote and mysterious. Go through a gate and when the path divides take the right-hand track, leading a little downhill. Then the path bears left along a more open hillside.

There was no sound as I walked along the hill, only birdsong; the cuckoo dominating as usual! I felt I was in another world, yet Fawley Refinery is barely two miles away. Such is the magic of the Forest. These woods were a favourite with W H Hudson. He writes about the Dark Water in *Hampshire Days*. 'In this wood I sought and found the stream well named the Dark Water; here it is grown over with old ivied oaks, with brambles and briars that throw long branches from side to side, making the almost hidden current in the deep shade look black; but when the sunlight falls on it the water is the colour of old sherry from the red soil it flows over.' When we come to the stream you will see it is just as he describes it but we will keep to our green track along the hillside as long as we can.

Keep to the main path ignoring all joining tracks from the left. You come to a crosstrack where a gravel track leads down to a bridge over the stream. Ignore this, go straight over the crosstrack, and follow the green path directly ahead. This soon leads down to a more secluded and lovely bridge over the Dark Water.

The stream flows as Hudson describes it, tree-shaded, between tall banks draped with ferns and wild flowers. I leaned on the rail of the wooden footbridge to watch the lights and reflections on the water and wonder, as always, at the neat way violets and primroses tuck themselves into sheltered spots between tree roots and into hollows along the bank. At one side, hazels, ferns, brackens and young pines crowd to the edge, but on the other the ground is more open and an occasional tall oak stands solemnly contemplating its own reflection in the water. Their large population of squirrels was confirmed by occasional flurries along the branches and glimpses of bright eyes watching me. W H Hudson tells this story about a squirrel who became crosser and crosser as he watched him. The squirrel was 'dancing about, whisking his tail, scolding in a variety of tones . . . and finally tearing off the loose bark with his little hands and teeth, and biting too at twigs and leaves so as to cause them to fall in showers. The little pot boils over in that way, and that's all there is to be said about it!'

From the bridge, climb through the pines to meet the gravel track we saw earlier just before a gate on the left. Turn left, go through the gate and leave the woods to come out onto the open heath. You are now on the southern edge of that part of Beaulieu Heath which lies to the east of the village, at King's Copse car park. Follow the gravel track across the heath. The minor road running from Hill Top above Beaulieu to Fawley is directly ahead. When you reach the minor road turn right and follow the road until you come to a point where green tracks lead left and right through Forestry Commission barriers.

Here you can add an optional mile to our walk if you wish. Turn left and follow the middle track which leads over the heath to some interesting Bronze Age tumuli. The heath beyond the tumuli is marshy and drains into Stoneyford Pond where I saw two magnificent Canada geese, so if you are a bird watcher then this extra mile is a must! As you follow the middle track over the heath from the gate by the road you will be able to see the distinct hummock shapes of the tumuli ahead. Follow the track until it brings you to these strange, isolated mounds. They are slowly being eroded but there is enough left of the largest one to give some idea of the original size of the burial places of those people who lived here two thousand years before our history was recorded.

Retrace your way back over the heath to the minor road again. On your way you might like to look for an interesting plant that C J Cornish mentions he saw here in 1894. He describes a kind of dwarf willow, creeping along the ground like ivy. To my delight I found some. They are perfect miniature willow bushes, studded with tiny satin globes like the common willow but growing in the horizontal position he describes.

When you reach the minor road turn left (if you did not visit the tumuli you keep straight on down the road) in the direction of Fawley, and walk downhill into the valley to cross the Dark Water again. Go past an inn on your right and climb the hill ahead. Look down over the shallow green meadows beside the Dark Water on your left. You will see they appear strangely ridged and embanked and that there appears to be the remains of a moat. This is a most historic part of the Forest. In medieval times Holbury Manor, held by the monks of Beaulieu, stood here. They made successive encroachments on to the Common land which led to protests from local people. But Holbury, the name means 'a fortress hollow', can be traced back to Roman times when it was a flourishing settlement. And earlier still, Mesolithic and Neolithic man — from 6000 to 2000 BC — roamed the Dark Water valley. Three hundred of their flint tools have been found here.

At the top of the hill you come to a crossroads. Our way lies down the narrow lane on the right leading back to King's Copse. But this time there is no heath to cross, only a pleasant English country lane bordered with bluebells leading to the wood. Turn left before the wood along the bridleway. (The lane straight on is a private drive leading through gates.) You walk with the trees on your right and farmland on your left. Where woods and cultivated land meet seems to be specially favourable for bluebells. They carpeted the woods, clustered thickly round the oak trees each side of the path, spilling over into the hedges and the fields. I had to pick my way to avoid crushing them.

Go through a gate and keep straight on slightly uphill. Go over a crosstrack and now keep on to follow the lovely, wide greenway ahead. The way bears right to take us back to Blackwell Common.

This interesting greenway, I believe, could be the route of an ancient British track, if not part of the track itself. It is very wide and raised and almost all grassed over. Here and there scattered oak trees growing on the track itself form a miniature woodland walk on each side. Unlike most woodland ways, this track is straight and determined in direction. To the east of Beaulieu Heath a known British track can be seen running through Fawley Inclosure and across the heath above Holbury. It was probably a trading route for, among other commodities, Cornish tin, long before the Romans came to build their roads in the first four centuries AD. The track would run from there quite close to the Dark Water to a trading port near Lepe or Stone Point. I believe that this greenway we are following could be another part of this old British track, a continuation of the remnant in Fawley Inclosure.

When you come to the edge of Blackwell Common you meet a crossing road. Go over the road and keep straight on over the heath along the line of an ancient earthwork to meet the road between Blackfield and Exbury where we began our walk. Turn right in the direction of Exbury for Blackwell Common car park and left to retrace your steps to Blackfield Crossroads. When you reach the main road, the bus stop for Southampton is a few yards on the left.

Walk 29

DIBDEN PURLIEU:
OF HATS AND NOADS AND ROMAN ROADS

Starting point: Oak Road car park, Dibden Purlieu. Bus: Heath Hotel, Dibden Purlieu roundabout.

Distance: 4 miles.

This short ramble will provide you with the most easily acquired potted history of the Forest. We begin on the Roman road mentioned in the title. This old road, possibly on the track of an earlier Celtic or Iron Age route, runs for part of its length beside the new Totton to Fawley road. Although its authenticity as a Roman road has been questioned, most authorities, including Margery, agree that it is genuine, connecting the important Forest port of Lepe (now decayed) with Southampton and Winchester in one direction, and Ringwood and the west in the other. In Roman times, and earlier, tin was brought from Cornwall down this road to be shipped from Lepe to the Isle of Wight and from there to France. Large masses of tin have been found close to the road.

We then go on to discover the noads, a Forest term for burial mounds raised in the Bronze Age, some three thousand years ago.

And then, the 'hats'. You will find 'hats' dotted about all over the Forest! This is not the result of unusually high winds but just another curious local name. Any eminent group of trees, perhaps strikingly tall or on a hill, is called a 'hat'. Sometimes the name remains after the original trees have been felled. The historian, Heywood Sumner, lists twenty-two 'hats' in the Forest. They have charmingly descriptive names and include Great Dark Hat and Little Dark Hat, Great Stubby

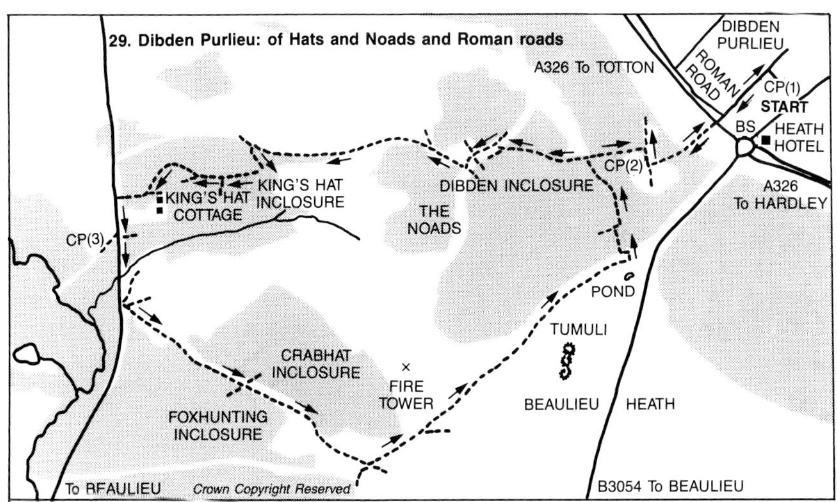

Additions to Key:
CP(1) *Oak Road car park, Dibden Purlieu*
CP(2) *Dibden Inclosure car park*
CP(3) *King's Hat car park*

For general Key see p. viii

Hat and Little Stubby Hat, Ashen's Hat, Black Bush Hat, and the much more impressive Cardinal's Hat. John Wise suggests the word may have had its origin in the high-crowned hats worn by the Puritans in the time of Charles I. We shall be walking through 'Kings Hat' and 'Crab Hat'.

The walk is about four miles round — perfect on a clear afternoon. There are splendid views and every variety of Forest scenery, oak woods, heathland, and green lawns.

Our starting point is Oak Road car park which is in Dibden Purlieu, about two and a half miles south-west of Hythe on the eastern boundary of the Forest. Driving from Totton, take the A326 (Fawley) road which bypasses Marchwood and Dibden Purlieu. Follow the bypass until you come to a roundabout and turn left following the sign for Dibden Purlieu. Immediately turn left again into Roman Road which runs parallel with the A326 at this point. A short way down Roman Road you will see a free car park sign pointing down Oak Road on your right. Follow the sign to the car park on the right, behind a new church. From the car park, turn left and walk back up Oak Road to Roman Road.

Across Roman Road you will see a track cutting through the gorse bushes. The track leads you over the grass verge to cross the A326 to a stile into Dibden Inclosure where we begin our walk.

If you come to Dibden Purlieu by bus from Hythe or Lymington, get off at the Heath Hotel by the roundabout. Cross the road leading to Dibden Purlieu and you will see Roman Road a little to your right. Walk down Roman Road to the top of Oak Road and on your left you will come to the little track through the gorse bushes. Follow the track over the grass verge. Cross the A326 and take the path which is almost straight ahead which leads to a stile.

Before you stretches a green lawn, backed by the trees of Dibden Inclosure. This is one of several man-made lawns in the Forest. These areas were seeded by the Forestry Commission by agreement with the commoners when new inclosures were made along this eastern boundary in 1959. Walk straight over the lawn. Go through another stile and down the path immediately ahead into the Inclosure through low-growing gorse and willows and young pines, interplanted with beech saplings. In a few yards you meet a track and see Dibden Inclosure car park ahead. Turn right and follow the track for a few yards until you come to a wide green way on your left. Turn left down this pleasant path. The young pines stand close like a green wall behind tall clumps of heather.

Keep straight on past all turnings until the wide way turns sharply left and ahead of you is a small gate. Keep straight on through the gate and — as happens so often in the Forest — you go through it into a different world! First a fringe of birches, their leaves and silver bark shimmering in the sunlight, then shadowy glades beneath the bent and hoary shapes of old oaks encircled by their hollies. Under the oaks, the sunlight splashes the lawns and grasses and brightens the red of last year's bracken, but among them stand enormous yews, darker than the hollies and under which nothing grows. But of all trees, the yew was once the most valued — and the most useful — perhaps that is why we see so few of them, except in churchyards. Their branches provided the pliant but powerful wood needed for the famous English longbow. Look for yews in these old woods, especially by pathways, as they were often planted as marker trees.

Ignore the first left turn as you leave the gate and walk on into the wood. The path forks here. Bear left and soon you come out of the trees onto a more open area of heathland. It is quite narrow and another old wood faces you on the other side. Keep straight on towards the second wood ignoring all right and left turns. As you come close to the wood, go straight over a crosstrack to a T-junction. Turn right, with the wood on your left, and follow the path as it leads you downhill. When the path divides keep to the left-hand way. Now you have a wonderful view westward over the Forest. You look down on the great woods around the upper reaches of the Beaulieu river, then on to a dense wall of woodland around Lyndhurst and beyond the Forest to a line of hills on the horizon, the chalklands of Dorset.

Our path leads us down the hillside and across a heath towards the right-hand corner of a dark line of pines which form the edge of King's Hat Inclosure. The track brings you close to the corner of King's Hat Inclosure which is on your left. The main track continues to the minor road which you will see over the heath ahead.

Our way is through the Inclosure itself so leave the main track when you reach the Inclosure corner, turn left and make your way to the Inclosure boundary fence. (There is no path at this point but in about thirty yards you are back on a good track.) With the Inclosure on your right follow the fence for about thirty yards to a gate on your right. Go through the gate and take the track ahead into these pinewoods.

After the oakwoods, so full of life, it is very still beneath the pines, the scented air hardly moves beneath the dense canopy of their boughs. Today, we are so used to pine trees that it seems almost unbelievable that, apart from the Scots pine and the yew, they are relative newcomers to our islands, planted in the New Forest as an experiment in 1776. As they became more widespread as a profitable quick growing tree, some people objected. This story is told by that delightful countryside writer, Richard Jefferies. On one occasion, when visiting the Forest, he talked with a woodman's wife, whose cottage lay away from the road surrounded by pine woods. He expressed his pleasure in her beautiful surroundings. 'I've had enough of it', was her reply, 'eighteen years; tis desprit lonesome. Past them ugly trees is the road, but you'll surely lose your way comin' back if you don't mark crosses with your sticks as ye go.' The King's Hat pines are surely not as depressing as that! Look for one group of really outstanding young pines, a vivid shade of emerald green.

Keep straight ahead when the main track turns left. When the path forks, bear right and follow the path as it bears left to bring you to a gravel crosstrack. On the left you will glimpse a cottage through the trees. Turn right to a gate leading to a minor road. Go through the gate out of King's Hat Inclosure.

Turn left and walk along the side of the road for about a quarter of a mile. Keep on past the turning to King's Hat car park on your right. You now come to the edge of King's Hat Inclosure and a narrow strip of open heath. It is important to get the right path here! Turn left but do not follow the path straight ahead which runs beside the Inclosure fence. Bear a few yards right towards Foxhunting Inclosure and you will come to a good path leading left over the heath. Turn left along this path so that you are walking with the heath on your left and the trees of Foxhunting Inclosure on your right. Soon the heath gives way to the trees of Crabhat Inclosure and you are walking through mixed woodlands of oaks, birches, sweet chestnuts and pines. When you come to a gravel track in a more open area go straight over and keep on up the slope opposite, following the path as it bears left to bring you onto the heath. We are now turning towards Dibden Purlieu, to make our way back across the eastern part of Beaulieu Heath. As you climb, a shallow valley runs beside you on the left. Then the heath widens into a large expanse of flat moorland that so delighted W H Hudson. In his *Hampshire Days* he writes of Beaulieu Heath: 'woods have a less enduring hold on the spirit than the open heath . . . it seems enough that it is open where the wind blows free, and there is nothing between us and the sun.' Contrast this with William Cobbett's view as he crossed Beaulieu Heath: 'A poorer spot than this New Forest there is not in all England', he grumbled, 'it's more barren and miserable than Bagshot Heath.' Of course, Cobbett was concerned about growing profitable crops, not watching wildlife — everything depends on your point of view!

Follow the track over the heath until you meet a path joining on the right (Fawley chimneys ahead on the horizon). Turn left. When the path forks, bear left again so that you are now facing Dibden Purlieu and walking in the direction of the B3054. Keep to the main track over all crossways.

As you walk back you will see all the different types of woodlands we have walked through neatly arranged beside you — the new pines of Dibden, the graceful varied outlines of the oak woods and the denser darker masses of the more mature pines. Close to the path on your right you will see three large barrows, or burial mounds. There are a hundred and seventy of these dotted all over the Forest. Constructed by the early Bronze Age people they are a reminder that men lived here over seventeen hundred years before the birth of Christ. Locally, they are known as the Noads.

Just before you reach the B3054 you will see a small pond on your right, and on your left an opening in the Inclosure fence. Turn left and go through the stile, then almost immediately left again for a few steps to a good path leading right into the Inclosure. When you come to a crossway, turn right for a few yards, then left again. Keep to this path, over all crossways, until you meet the very wide, embanked path we followed from Dibden Inclosure car park at the beginning of our walk. Turn right to rejoin our original route and follow it round the car park, then through the gorse bushes on the left, over the lawn and back to the A326. Cross the main road and walk down Oak Road to the car park, or turn left down Roman Road for the bus stop in Dibden Purlieu.

The name is interesting, reflecting the people of the Forest and their livelihood. 'Dibden' is Saxon meaning a deep wooded valley. 'Purlieu' is from Norman-French; *Pur*—exempt, *lieu*—place. This was land on the edge of the Forest that at some time in the past had been wrongfully included within the Forest perambulation, or official boundaries. Subsequently the error had been corrected and the land disafforested; it became no longer subject to the Forest Laws and could be farmed.

Walk 30

NEW FOREST MAGIC:
HATCHET POND AND STUBBS WOOD

Starting point: Hatchet Pond car park. Bus: Hatchett Gate, near Beaulieu.

Distance: 4 miles.

I have placed this walk last in my Companion to the Forest because, more than any other of my rambles, it gives me the greatest pleasure. If you walk in the Forest I am sure you will agree that here is a kind of quiet magic, the result perhaps of the Forest's timelessness, peace and unassuming beauty. I feel this magical quality most strongly in the great oak woods where we find the survivors of so many centuries of our history. This walk takes us to one of these, Stubbs Wood, which, in spite of its unromantic name, is full of enchantment. We pause for a while beside a pretty stretch of water, Hatchet Pond, and on our way to the wood, take a closer look at the way traditional Forest cottages were built. The distance round is about four miles.

We begin our walk from the car park on the northern side of Hatchet Pond. To get here by car, take the Beaulieu road from Lyndhurst, the B3056. Past the turning for Beaulieu village, bear right along the B3054 in the direction of Brockenhurst. After about a mile and a half you come to a junction with the B3055. Keep straight on down this road for only a short distance and you will see the car park on the left, beside Hatchet Pond. You can catch a bus from Lymington or Hythe and alight at Hatchett Gate, only a few yards away from the car park. A nice day out would be to take the ferry from Southampton to Hythe, then the bus from the ferry landing to Hatchett Gate.

It was early in April when we stood by Hatchet Pond. This area has practically no protection from the winds that blow unchecked across Beaulieu Heath, a fact that explains the formation of the lake. Heywood Sumner, a Forest historian, tells us that an old map of the Forest does not show the present crescent-shaped sheet

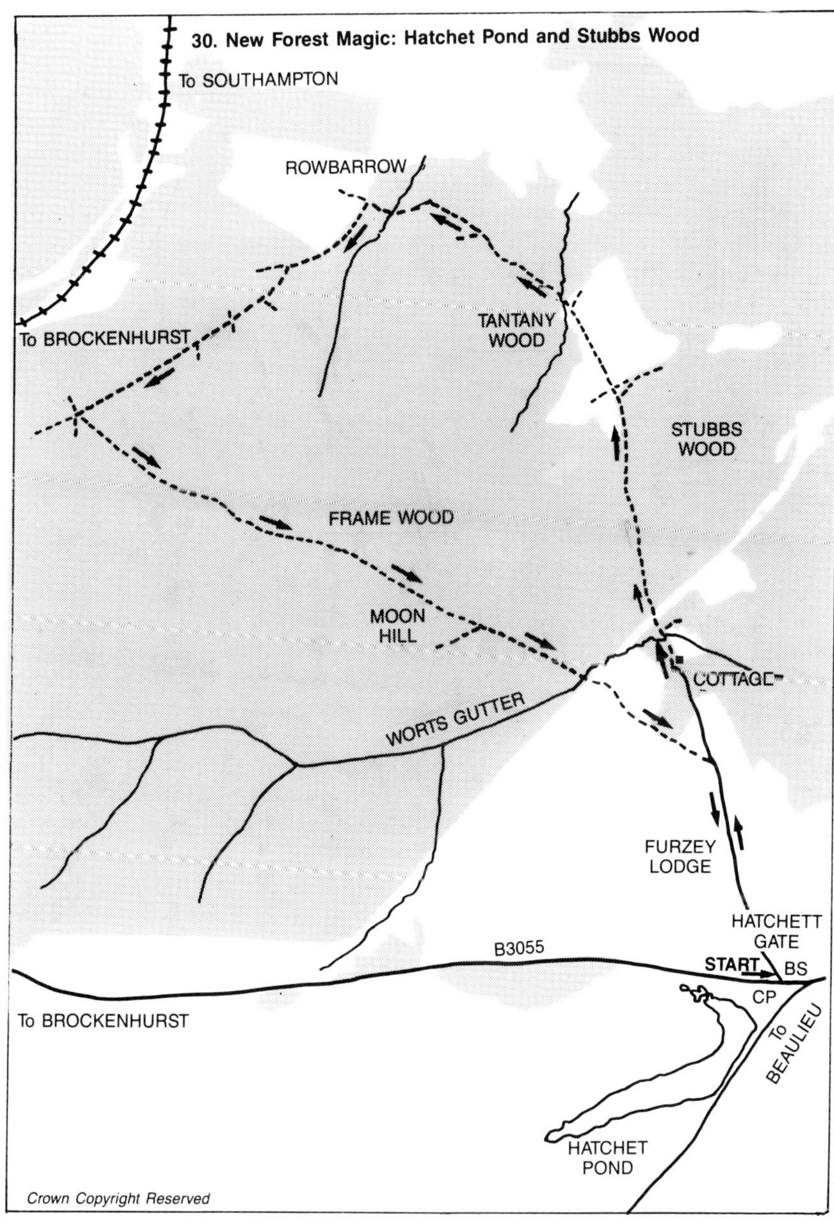

Additions to Key:
CP *Hatchet Pond car park*

For general Key see p. viii

of water but on its site indicates several circles marked as 'old marl pits'. He suggests that the action of the wind on the water which collected in the pits wore away their edges so they joined to become one pond. One of the commoners' rights was to dig marl from the Forest earth to improve the quality of their agricultural land.

Hatchet Pond derives its name from 'hatch', an old word for a gate. Hatchett Gate cottage stands on the edge of the heath where the open Forest gives way to the farming lands, privately owned, around Beaulieu. The straggle of houses east of the pond follow the boundary line. They are now called East Boldre but the old name for them was Beaulieu Rails and cottagers here still say they live 'under the rails'. Old ideas and customs linger in the Forest. The village inn in East Boldre is called the Turf Cutter's Arms, recalling another of the commoners' rights, the right to cut peat on the principle of 'cut one, leave two'. On the wall opposite the bar are two peat-cutting spades with their slightly-curved handles and leaf-shaped blades. The original Turf Cutter's Arms was an ancient thatched cottage with a path leading from it to the coast. This was a favourite smugglers' run. They hid their contraband in the oven!

To begin our walk, turn right from the car park along the B3055. A few yards further on you will see a lane leading left over the heath past some cottages marked on the map as Furzey Lodge. Follow this lane, heading north. Some of the cottages here are very old. They show the traditional way of building a home in the Forest with mud walling, known as 'dob'. Heywood Sumner explains how they were made. Clayey loam with small stones in it was mixed with heather, rushes or straw which was thoroughly puddled into the mass with tramping. This was 'dobbed' or bonded by the builder with a three-pronged fork in successive layers on stone or brick foundations. Only two feet could be raised at a time, and each layer had to be left for ten days to dry out. Finished walls were often coated with plaster or pebbledash. As late as 1923 local craftsmen were known to be raising good dob walls.

Keep straight on past a joining lane on the left which leads to a small car park. When the lane forks carry straight on downhill to the left of the last pretty cottage. Follow the path past a Forestry Commission barrier. Ahead, several tiny streams curve round the tree roots to form a watersmeet. Cross by the wooden footbridge and you will see our path leading over a lawn then uphill into Stubbs Wood.

Follow the path into this most enchanting of oak woods and keep to the main path straight ahead through the trees. It was so quiet as we walked through the glades canopied by the branches of ancient oaks, our footsteps muffled by the soft green moss, that we felt we should talk in whispers! The only sounds were the chorus of birdsong and the patter of last year's dried leaves as the wind blew them in drifts between the tree roots. All the oak trees have their own peculiarities. Some have fern gardens in the hollows of their branches, some appear to be sprouting out of the top of holly thickets and others have almost vanished underneath thick coils of honeysuckle and ivy.

Gradually the oaks thin out and you come to a glade. The path is not very clear at this point and make certain you find the correct path. As you enter the glade, bear a little left (not sharp left) to leave a conspicuous clump of holly and oak trees on your right. Now you walk with heathland on your right and an old oak wood edged with silver birches on your left. Keep straight on past a joining path on the right, into Tantany Wood and cross a tiny stream. Follow the path ahead as it winds through this beautiful wood of oaks and beeches.

These are just the kinds of trees you would expect to find in a wood called 'Tantany' which is a colloquial version of St. Anthony. The wood is dedicated to him because he was the patron Saint of pigs who thrive on acorns and beech mast.

The trees thin and the lovely green path now winds ahead of you through the bracken dotted with birches and oaks. After about a quarter of a mile the path divides. Bear right, slightly downhill to meet a joining track on the right. Bear a little left to cross a stream. Walk on for only a few yards towards a wide heath you will see ahead. As you reach the edge of the heath do not follow a very obvious path leading straight ahead, but turn left through the outlying trees of Tantany Wood which is now on your left.

Go through the gate directly ahead into the shade of pinewoods. They seem dark after the oak wood glades but their scent, especially after rain, is delicious! Bear left when you come to a Y-junction and keep straight on into Frame Wood down the wide track. Pass all joining tracks on the left until in a little less then a mile you come to a point where five tracks (including the one we are following) meet.

Our way is down the green ride on your immediate left. This soon leads you out of the pines into the mixed woodlands of Frame Wood. We are heading straight back for Furzey Lodge and aim to join our original road in front of the cottages by a track entering from the left. Go through an inclosure gate and follow the path through a lovely wood of old oaks and hollies. Keep to the main track at all divisions (the left-hand path). When you go through another gate you follow a green path through a young pine wood. This leads you to a gravel track which curves away to your right. Carry straight on downhill to cross a bridge over a tiny stream — named after the Old English word for plants 'Worts Gutter' — and go through the gate out of the wood. Now you have a complete change of scene. You are standing in a shallow heath-covered valley and our path winds uphill through the gorse ahead. Climb the hill following this path to join the road you took at the beginning of the walk. Turn right and walk the short distance back to Hatchet Pond.

<h1 style="text-align:center">· BOOK LIST ·</h1>

The New Forest John Wise. First published 1883, new edition 1971. SR Publications.

The New Forest Heywood Sumner. First published 1924, new edition 1972. Dolphin Press.

Hampshire Days W H Hudson. First published 1906, new edition 1973. Barry Shurlock.

Remarks on Forest Scenery W Gilpin. First published 1791, new edition. Richmond Publications.

Rural Rides W Cobbett ed C D and M Cole. 1930. Macdonald and Jane's.

Gypsies of the New Forest and Other Tales H E J Gibbens. 1909.

The New Forest C J Cornish.

Boldre: Its Parish, Church and Inhabitants W F Perkins. 1935.

The New Forest, An Ecological History C Tubbs. 1968. David & Charles.

A Hampshire Treasury M Green. 1972. Winton Publications.

It Happened in Hampshire Published by the Hampshire Federation of Women's Institutes.

New Forest Commoners Anthony Pasmore.

British Folk Customs Christina Hole. 1976. Hutchinson.

Sketches of Life, Character and Scenery in the New Forest Philip Klitz.

I have also found the Guides published by the Forestry Commission useful, particularly those to the Forest Trails.

Note: *not all the above titles are currently in print. If you can't get a particular book from your local bookseller, your local library may well have a copy which can be used for reference purposes.*

• INDEX •